British Labour and the Russian

The Leeds Convention

An expanded centenary edition
Edited by Janet Douglas and Christian Høgsbjerg
With Ken Coates' original Introduction

The Russian Revolution.

NATIONAL LABOUR AND SOCIALIST
CONVENTION
& DEMONSTRATION

Convened by the United Socialist Council of the
Independent Labour Party & British Socialist Party

COLISEUM, LEEDS,

Sunday, June 3rd, 1917.

**FIRST SESSION - 10-30 a.m. to 12-45 p.m.
SECOND SESSION 2-15 p.m. to 5 p.m.
Demonstration, 7 p.m.** (Seats reserved until 6-45).

BRING THIS WITH YOU.

*[Leeds Convention ticket, reproduced courtesy of the People's History
Museum, Manchester, with thanks to Darren Treadwell]*

SPOKESMAN
2017

An expanded centenary edition of
British Labour and the Russian Revolution:
The Leeds Convention: A Report from the Daily Herald
with an Introduction by Ken Coates
Published by The Bertrand Russell Peace Foundation Limited
for *The Spokesman,* Nottingham, 1974

Dedicated to the memory of Matthew Caygill (1955-2016)

Published in 2017 by
Spokesman
Russell House
Bulwell lane
Nottingham NG6 0BT
UK

Phone 0115 9708318
Fax 0115 9420433
www.spokesmanbooks.com

A catalogue record is available from the British Library
ISBN 978 0 85124 865 3

Printed in Nottingham by Russell Press (www.russellpress.com)

Contents

Acknowledgements

Our thanks to Iain Dalton, David Howell, Michael Meadowcroft, Graham Mustin, Stuart Stanton, Darren Treadwell, and to the staff of the British Library, Local and Family History Library at Leeds Central Library, and the People's History Museum. We are particularly indebted to the staff of the Modern Records Centre at the University of Warwick for their work digitising and making available online many of the original documents reproduced in this volume. We would also like to thank Tony Simpson and the team at Spokesman Books for all their work and support for this project.

Introduction

by Ken Coates

The Leeds Convention of June 1917 has been described by Ralph Miliband as "perhaps the most remarkable gathering of the period."[1] The description seems to be a fair one.

To bring together 1,150 delegates, and to accommodate on one platform such assorted characters as Ramsay Macdonald, Philip Snowden, W.C. Anderson, Tom Mann, Bob Smillie, Ben Tillett, Robert Williams and Bertrand Russell was no small feat of organisation for the fragmented British left. Of course, the United Socialist Council, which convened the meeting, was reacting to the altogether unprecedented stimulus of the Russian Revolution.

The United Socialist Council had been formed in July 1913, when the Socialist International Bureau convened a meeting of British socialist organisations to discuss the possibilities of unity. Vandervelde and Huysmans had attended for the Bureau, and delegates had been assembled from the Independent Labour Party, the Fabians, and the British Socialist Party.

J. Ramsey MacDonald:
"kept telling long Scotch stories"

Dora Montefiore:
"one of the greatest tragedies of the war is to see the idealist laying down his life for a peace that is to be arranged by the materialist"

The spokesmen of the International had recommended a dual solution to British disunity: the I.L.P. and the B.S.P. should fuse, and the B.S.P. should affiliate to the Labour Party, following which, pending further developments towards unity, a United Socialist Council was to be set up comprising all three bodies, under the chairmanship of Beatrice Webb.[2] At a subsequent conference attended by many international delegates, the B.S.P. put forward four conditions for unity with the I.L.P. Keir Hardie agreed to three of these: that the party should be free to proclaim its socialist goal, that it should recognise the existence of the class war, and that it should be free to carry on extra-Parliamentary activity including intervention in trade union struggles. The fourth, that B.S.P. parliamentary candidates should stand on an explicitly socialist ticket, was met by Hardie with a compromise proposal that the United Socialist Council should ask its members to request the Labour Party to amend its constitution to permit candidates to describe themselves as "Labour and Socialist".

The next year, 1914, the B.S.P. held a referendum which revealed agreement on affiliation.[3] Application was made, and accepted unanimously at the 1916 Labour Party Conference. Meantime, the war had sharpened the divergences between the revolutionary policies of the B.S.P. and the pacifist outlook of the majority of the I.L.P., to say nothing of the Fabian view, so that the United Socialist Council was shelved by the last two bodies. It took the Russian Revolution of March 1917 to bring revolutionaries and reformists close enough together to permit the B.S.P. and the I.L.P. to revive the United Socialist Council, and convene the Leeds Convention.

Years later, Aneurin Bevan was to speak, at the Labour Party Conference, immediately after his resignation from the Attlee cabinet, of the impact of the Russian Revolution on the British workers.

"I am now 53 years of age. I was coming to adult life at the end of the 1914-18 war. I remember so well what happened when the Russian revolution occurred. I remember the miners, when they heard that the Tsarist tyranny had been overthrown, rushing to meet each other in the streets with tears streaming down their cheeks, shaking hands and saying; 'At last it has happened.' Let us remember in 1951 that the revolution of 1917 came to the working class of Great Britain, not as a social disaster, but as one of the most emancipating events in the history of mankind. Let us also remember that the Soviet revolution would not have been so distorted, would not have ended in tyranny, would not have resulted in dictatorship, would not now be threatening the peace of mankind, had it not been for the behaviour of Churchill, and the Tories at that time. Do not forget that in the early days when that great mass of backward people were trying to find their way to the light, were trying to lift themselves from age-long penury and oppression, they were diverted from their objectives and thrown back into the darkness, not by the malignancy of Stalin at first, but by the action and malignancy of Churchill, the City of London, New York and all the rest of the capitalist world.

Ernest Bevin:
"The Platform says: 'the tide is on the rise for us.' For Whom? The professional politicians of the Labour Party"

7

The reasons for fear in the world at the moment have never come from the poor people, whenever they are trying to improve their lot. They have always come from those who are trying to hold them down. That is why I am frightened at the prospect of what may happen in this election. I am really frightened. We have been for this period of 30 years reaping the bitter fruits of the failure of the British working class to put Bob Smillie, Lansbury, and men like that, in power in 1918 and 1919. The responsibility lies on us. We failed. Because we failed, as a result of our political insecurity, we find that great parts of the world that ought to be contributing to the prosperity of mankind are sources of fear of war."[4]

Bevan's emotion, created in the turmoil of his own bitter struggle of 1951, provoked him into a stark recapitulation of the hopes and disappointments of *his* lifetime. That lifetime was a part of the hard life experience of the British working class, which knows many years of disappointment and yet can remember a few brilliant flashes of hope. No flash was ever brighter than this, the dawn of the Revolution in Russia: and the Leeds Convention shows in the sharpest relief how British socialists saw it.

There can be no doubt that the Convention excited those who participated in it. John Paton, later to become an organiser of the I.L.P., wrote in his memoirs that the delegates "spent a deliriously happy weekend in bold talk of what they hoped to do. There had even been mention of the new Russian device of Workers' and Soldiers' Councils."[5]

Mrs. Dora Montefiore, the women's suffrage leader who helped to found the British Communist Party, unwittingly captured the great aspirations of the Convention in her description of the organisational difficulties it encountered and overcame: "This Leeds demonstration was so boycotted by the possessing class that we delegates on arrival at Leeds station found that all hotels had refused to receive us. In consequence our own Leeds comrades had rapidly organised a reception committee who were on the platform of the station, and directed us to the houses of the various comrades who were offering hospitality. This appeared to me to be an example of rapid and efficient organised Labour, the possibilities of which might, in the future, have far-reaching results."[6] The fiery content of the speeches might properly be judged in this context.

But not all the delegates suffered quite so drastic a boycott. Lady Constance Malleson, who was at the time very closely involved with Bertrand Russell in his pacifist campaigns, has recorded her own memories:

"We went from Cambridge to Leeds — where a conference was being held with the idea of establishing Workers' and Soldiers' Councils after the pattern of those in Russia. We joined a crowded train at Peterborough and we travelled up to Leeds in a third class carriage with about ten others: Ramsay MacDonald, Gerald Gould and Edgar Lansbury (a most delightful pair), B.R., etc. It was very hot — and Ramsay

8

MacDonald kept telling long Scotch stories. On our arrival at Leeds, the hotels did their best to refuse us accommodation . . . The waiters slapped our food in front of us anyhow. The crowd hissed as we went through the streets to the conference. Some of the children threw stones. There were a lot of police about. I had a seat at the very back of the gallery, right at the top. Russell got up to speak. I couldn't see him, but I knew it could be no one else − because he always got a bigger reception than anyone. There weren't many men over military age who thought it worthwhile to come out hot and strong against the war. B.R. spoke of Allen (whom we had just seen sentenced at Newhaven to a further term of imprisonment) and at Allen's name there was a burst of applause that must have lasted fully a minute. It was rather fine."[7]

Russell was somewhat unkinder about MacDonald's jokes: he characterised them as "so dull that it was almost impossible to know when the point had been reached."[8] Nevertheless, MacDonald's oratory was not inhibited by the glum reception his anecdotes had received on the voyage up to Leeds. Leonard Woolf, another participant, reported it ironically, but not without sympathy:

"MacDonald, who exactly 20 years later was to end his political career widely discredited as the rather pitiful prisoner of his aristocratic and Tory allies, moved the first resolution: 'Hail! The Russian Revolution.' At one time I knew Ramsay fairly well and later on shall have more to say about him; here it is sufficient to say that he was in his element in 1917, a period of his career in which he was a rebel and pacifist in the political wilderness, addressing this immense sympathetic audience in Leeds. For he was a fine figure of a man, with a handsome face to satisfy a maiden's or a hairdresser's dream, with a golden bell-like bull-like voice which said nothing at such inordinate length and so persuasively that he could always get a Labour audience shouting with enthusiasm − at least until August 23, 1931, when most Labour people thought he had deserted them for the Londonderrys and the Tories."[9]

To hear MacDonald inveighing against "all forms of political, economic and imperialist oppression and exploitation", was not a new experience in 1917. What *was* new, was to hear him call "Let us lay down our own terms, make our own proclamations, establish our own diplomacy, see to it that we have our own international meetings."[10] Leonard Woolf also recollected, rather vividly, two other resolutions which were approved during the sessions:

"The second resolution, proposed by Snowden, pledged 'ourselves to work for . . . a peace without annexations or indemnities and based on the rights of nations to decide their own affairs'. The third resolution was on Civil Liberty, proposed by Ammon, a trade unionist Labour M.P., and Mrs. Despard. Mrs. Despard was a well known suffragette. A very frail elderly lady, she had, I think, only recently come out of gaol;

Tom Mann:
"Let us urge France to do the same thing, but before we cry out to France, let us do it ourselves"

she was given a tremendous reception by the meeting. Clio, the cynical Muse of History, who presumably knows both the future and the past, if she listened to our resolution, must have smiled grimly at the irony of facts. For this is what we voted unanimously:

> This Conference calls upon the Government of Great Britain to place itself in accord with the democracy of Russia by proclaiming its adherence to and determination to carry into immediate effect a charter of liberties establishing complete political rights for all men and women, unrestricted freedom of the press, freedom of speech, a general amnesty for all political and religious prisoners, full rights of industrial and political association, and the release of labour from all forms of compulsion and restraint.

Another frail figure received an enthusiastic welcome when he supported the resolution in the precise, clipped, aristocratic voice which, I always think, Bertie Russell must have inherited from his 18th-century Whig ancestors. I wonder how many of us who cheered Bertie and the resolution remember what we had voted for when the democracy of Russia was embodied in first Lenin, Trotsky, and Dzerzhinsky, and later Stalin"[11]

More unusual still, as Ralph Miliband stresses, was the fourth resolution of the Convention, moved by W.C. Anderson and Robert Williams. Williams, in seconding, speaks out for the dictatorship of the proletariat. "We are competent to speak in the name of our own class, and damn the Constitution . . . If you are really sincere in sending greetings to Russia, I say to you: 'Go thou

10

and do likewise'." Even Anderson, in this ferment, burst out: "if revolution be that we are not going to put up in the future with what we have put up with in the past, then the sooner we have revolution in this country the better."

As Miliband rightly observes, "The Leeds Convention had fortuitously brought together the revolutionaries and the constituionalists. But the gulf between them remained as profound as it ever had been and the instauration of the Bolshevik regime in November 1917 only served to widen that gulf."[12] This would have been clear to many of the Leeds delegates, as they cheered Williams' rousing speech. The parliamentarians were caught off-balance, but their position was still plain to those who read the newspapers.

For instance, barely one month before the Convention, the mover of the fourth resolution, the same W.C. Anderson, MP, had addressed the House of Commons. Here is what he said, and very revealing it is:

> "The trouble is there. You have got to get through the trouble. You will either have to get through with wise guidance on the part of the local trade union leaders, or if they have nothing to do with it and wash their hands of it, then it will undoubtedly get into the hands of people in whose hands settlement will be much more difficult, if not altogether impossible. If there are some extremists in the trade union movement, as I have no doubt there are, I do say this that the best friends that the extremists have got . . . are the Government. The Government is creating

Mrs. Despard:
"We did not have much liberty before the war, but now . . . we are allowing all our liberties to be taken away."

11

Bertrand Russell
*"it is possible for the individual
to stand . . . against the whole
might of the organised state."*

extremists all the time. The extremists would have no power but for the
grievances the Government are creating, they are giving the extremists
their opportunity. Therefore the best way if you wish to deal with extremists is to remove discontent and try to get a better relationship established between the Government and organized labour throughout the
country. I ask the Hon. Member whether he has yet reached any proposals with regard to the matter. Does he propose to close the door, or is
he going to try to meet the views of the men? The men say that they
wish you to honour what they regard as two undertakings on the part
of the Government. Did you give those undertakings? And if you give
those undertakings, do you mean to honour them? Those are quite
clear, straight definite issues. Let me say in conclusion that I have been
very much astonished indeed, in visiting various places recently at seeing
a feeling springing up in this country which I did not believe possible,
that is a deeper revolutionary feeling springing up among many of the
workmen of this country. The old policy on the part of rulers there
used to be that when grievances reached a certain point concessions
were made, and very largely the steam taken out of the movement, so
far as the extreme elements were concerned. What you are now doing
by coercive laws, by repressive laws, by the penal side of the Munitions
Act, and so on, is to try to dam up all the current of discontent, but
that current will not be dammed up. I do assure you you will be astonished, and unless you are very careful you will bring the country to
the very verge of revolution. Only a week ago, I saw 70,000 people:
the estimate was made not by any labour people, but by one of the

local newspapers – march through the streets of Glasgow with bands and banners, every one of the members of that procession wearing the revolutionary colours. That is an amazing thing to happen in a city like Glasgow. I say that to a very large extent it is the policy of the Government that is responsible for that. Now you have to choose whether you are going to apply increasing repressions to these men, or whether you are going to try to establish confidence and a sense of freedom. That is really the issue. I hope that in what I have said this afternoon I have avoided anything that would increase passion, anything likely to make matters worse. I do hope the reply we may receive from the Government Front Bench will be an answer that will help to tone down or to remove that unrest that undoubtedly now exists."[13]

If this sums up precisely the true attitude of the reformist leaders of the movement, Anderson's subsequent speech at Leeds also reveals the extent to which they felt they were losing their grip.

Their audience at Leeds, from Trades Councils, shop stewards' organisations, and other grass-roots organs of Labour opinion and activity, was gathering an increasingly explicit experience against which to evaluate Russian events.

The drive to find cannon-fodder from the factories, coupled with the intensification of dilution, was producing a veritable explosion of feeling among the skilled trade unionists. Highly trained men, tied to their jobs, found themselves working for wages considerably lower than the earnings

William Gallacher:
"This conference seems to be agreed that the Russian Revolution is definitely settled, but is it?"

of semi-skilled and unskilled dilutees, who were able to benefit from piece-work rates designed to stimulate maximum war-time productivity. These skilled men provided the impetus to form a nation-wide Shop Stewards' Movement, which was already producing a heated agitation when the March Revolution erupted in Russia. After March strikes flared out all over Britain, culminating in a widespread movement of stoppages triggered off by a dispute at Rochdale on the issues of the extension of dilution from war work to commercial work, and the exemption of skilled men from conscription. Manchester, Sheffield, Coventry, Birmingham, London, Woolwich, Leicester, Rugby, Derby, Liverpool, Birkenhead, Leeds and Newcastle all joined in, so that at the height of the dispute a quarter of a million engineers were involved, all over England. (Significantly, the Clyde was not concerned: the repressions there had taken effect.) The "May Strikes" gave a big fillip to the drive for an explicit organisation of shop stewards and workers' committees, and on May 15th a national delegate conference of strike committees was held in London. Its procla-mations were suppressed by the censor, and three days later its leaders were arrested. At this point the stewards sought aid from the national leaderships of their unions, who provided a formula for the release of the arrested men, which was based on a return to work. The Government thus regained control, and the strike was defeated although in some areas it continued for a week or two. But the shop stewards learned the obvious lesson: that without co-ordination they were powerless. Soon after the Leeds Convention, the first fully representative national conference of shop stewards was convened in Manchester, on August 18th and 19th. This was obviously profoundly influenced by the deliberations of the Leeds meeting.[14] Not only were leaders like Arthur McManus, Willie Gallacher and J.T. Murphy involved in both gatherings, but the content of the fourth resolution of the Convention was more and more appealing to the militants who were gathering around the shop stewards' banners.

It was this which worried authority. Graubard[15] quotes a fascinating interview between Will Thorne and King George V:

"The King seemed greatly disturbed about the famous Leeds Con-ference, and asked me if I knew anything about it. I said, "Yes, I knew all about it. I've read all the proceedings." I also told him about the telegram that had been sent from the Conference that made the Russians think we were spies, and he was amused at my story of the incidents that had happened over the message. 'Do you think that any ill will come from this Conference at Leeds and the decisions that were made there?' the King asked me, 'No,' I said, 'I've seen these things happen before many times in days gone by, and in my humble judge-ment there will never be a physical violent revolution in this country. But there will have to be many political and industrial chages within the course of the next few years.' This seemed to relieve his mind, and he spoke to me in a most homely and pleasant way. I was very pleased."[16]

The historians have tended to accept, with relief, Thorne's view of the Convention. Alan Bullock, in his life of Bevin, speaks of it as "a preview of the British Left between the wars, anarchical, Utopian, already fascinated by and profoundly ignorant of the Russian experience."[17]

Middlemass, in his study of the I.L.P., writes of Bevin's tactless and uncouth intervention as an "attempt to restore sanity", and adds that "the enthusiasm of Snowden and MacDonald . . . left the Marxist delegates Gallacher and MacManus with nothing to add.[18] This was certainly not Gallacher's view. In the first volume of his autobiography he scornfully condemns the interventions of MacDonald and Snowden as a "regular orgy of generalities on the beauty and holiness of bourgeois democracy."[19] Gallacher, incidentally, denies that the record of the Convention contains any accurate report of his speech. Far from having "added nothing" he claims to have advanced a programme of revolutionary activities for the new National Committee which the Convention was to establish. He chides the *Daily Herald* for giving "column after column to MacDonald, Snowden and company", while he was was accorded only one inch of space. (Gallacher, incidentally, wrongly states that George Lansbury was present at the Convention. Although the *Herald* actively promoted it, and Lansbury was most keen that it should succeed, he was too ill to attend, as the record makes plain.) Since the report of the Convention which we are producing is reprinted from the *Herald's* account, Gallacher's complaint is worthy of notice by those who have relied upon its evidence.

The fate of the Convention, its lapse from the status of central importance, accorded to it by so many socialists in the years after 1917, to a mere episode among the footnotes of Labour history, is part of the history of a whole succession of defeats which the Labour Movement encountered from 1920 onwards. But the episode occurred, and it is instructive to remember it.

FOOTNOTES

1. Ralph Miliband — *Parliamentary Socialism*, p. 55.
2. Who was very flattered to be chosen, according to Margaret Cole — cf. *The Story of Fabian Socialism*, p. 170.
3. For an account of this episode, see Lee and Archbold — *Social Democracy in Britain*, pp. 210-17.
   See also Morton and Tate — *British Labour Movement*, pp. 244-5.
4. Labour Party Annual Conference Report, 1951, p. 194.
5. John Paton, *Proletarian Pilgrimage*, p. 299.
6. Dora Montefiore, *From a Victorian to a Modern*, p. 194.
7. Constance Malleson, *After Ten Years*, London, Cape, 1931, pp. 113-4
8. Bertrand Russell, *Autobiography* Volume 2, Allen & Unwin, p. 31.
9. Leonard Woolf, *Beginning Again*, Hogarth Press, 1964, p. 212.

10. See MacDonald's speech, below.
11. *Ibid*, pp. 212-3.
12. Miliband, *op. cit.*, p. 56-7.
13. Hansard, 14th May, 1917. This most revealing quotation was brought to my attention by Anthony Topham, who also provided the text of the pamphlet which is reproduced here, below.
14. For a detailed account of the disputes in engineering, see J.T. Murphy, *Preparing for Power*, pp. 135-60.
15. Graubard, *British Labour and the Russian Revolution*, p. 41.
16. Thorne, *My Life's Battles*, p. 195.
17. Bullock, *Ernest Bevin*, Volume One, p. 75.
18. Middlemass, *The Clydesiders* — a left wing struggle for Parliamentary Power, p. 75.
19. Gallacher, *Revolt on the Clyde*, p. 149.

The Road to the Leeds Convention

Janet Douglas and Christian Høgsbjerg

There was considerable sympathy in Britain for the February Revolution of 1917 in Russia, which overthrew centuries of Tsarist despotism, not least amongst liberals and socialists, many of whom had personal connections with Russian émigrés. As early as 1890, 'The Society of the Friends of Russian Freedom' had been established with its own monthly newsletter *Free Russia*.[1] The revolutionary process in Russia during the events of February 1917 saw not only the end of the detested emperor Tsar Nicholas II but also the rebirth of the soviets - workers' and soldiers' councils. The soviets were multi-party councils of elected workers and soldiers, organs of direct democracy first seen in the 1905 Russian Revolution, but rather than try and rule in their own name after February they voted to give formal power to a new Provisional Government in the parliament (the Duma).

The response of Lloyd George's Coalition Government and the wider British ruling class to the February Revolution in Russia might be best summed up by a resolution submitted to the House of Commons and moved by the Conservative leader, Bonar Law:

> That this House sends to the Duma its fraternal greetings, and tenders to the Russian people its heartiest congratulations upon the establishment among them of free institutions in full confidence that they will lead not only to the rapid and happy progress of the Russian nation but to the prosecution with renewed steadfastness and vigour of the war against the stronghold of an autocratic militarism which threatens the liberty of Europe.

Pro-war Labour politicians like Will Thorne and the Leeds East MP James O'Grady, who were used by the Lloyd George Government as Labour personalities in the wider war effort, were duly sent to Petrograd with, in Bonar Law's words, 'the one object of encouraging the present Russian Government in the prosecution of the War. The British Government are satisfied that they will serve the purpose.'[2]

Yet by 1917, the mood among ordinary people in Britain was turning against the war and militarism, and for many the Russian Revolution was a beacon of hope that the bloodshed and war might be brought to

17

an end, given the Petrograd Soviet had called for world leaders to negotiate a peaceful settlement. By March 1917 there had already been mass meetings held in London in solidarity with the Russian Revolution, such as the 7,000 strong rally in the Great Assembly Hall on Mile End Road on 24 March 1917 which heard speeches from representatives of Russian socialist groups, from Robert Williams of the Transport Workers' Union, as well as from Edwin C. Fairchild and Joseph Fineberg, both of the British Socialist Party (BSP). This meeting set up a 'League of Rights for Soldiers and Sailors' to argue for pension rights on the grounds that 'fit to fight, fit to pension'.[3] This rally was followed on 31 March 1917 by an even greater rally held at the Royal Albert Hall in London, hailing 'Russia Free!' with an estimated 12,000 in attendance and a further five thousand turned away. The speakers here included not only Robert Williams again but also George Lansbury of the Labour Party and editor of *The Herald* (who acted as chairman), the socialist journalist Henry Woodd Nevinson, the novelist Israel Zangwill, the trade union leaders Robert Smillie and Albert Bellamy (of the National Union of Railwaymen), the suffragist Maude Royden, Commander Josiah Wedgwood, a Liberal MP; Arthur Lynch, the Irish Parliamentary Party MP, Labour MP William Crawford Anderson, Charlotte Despard and Bertrand Russell. This mass rally, described by *The Herald* as 'The Revolt at the Albert Hall', ended with the singing of *The Red Flag*.[4] The following resolution was passed:

> This Meeting sends joyful congratulations to the Democrats of Russia, and calls upon the Governments of Great Britain and of every country, neutral and belligerent alike, to follow the Russian example by establishing Industrial Freedom, Freedom of Speech and the Press, the Abolition of Social, Religious and National inequalities, an immediate Amnesty for Political and Religious offences, and Universal Suffrage.

A booklet of the proceedings, 'Russia Free!', was published by *The Herald*.[5] May Day rallies across the country were popular events held in solidarity with the Russian Revolution. As Alan Clinton and George Myers noted,

> On May Day 70,000 demonstrators in Glasgow called for 'the over-throw of capitalism and the establishment of a co-operative commonwealth as the

only solution to poverty and unemployment'. Thousands in Manchester cheered and applauded Robert Williams, leader of the Transport Workers' Federation, when he said that revolutions like charity begin at home'. In Liverpool 150 Russian sailors headed the demonstration and received a tumultuous reception at the meeting afterwards. In London nearly 50,000 marched in solidarity with the revolution, against conscription, for votes for all and for an immediate peace.[6]

In Victoria Square, Leeds, on Sunday 6 May 1917, around 1,000 trade unionists and socialists took part in a May Day rally in support of the overthrow of Tsardom in Russia, while on the same day 'women pacifists' held a rally for peace on Woodhouse Moor. The Leeds May Day rally discussed and voted for the following resolution in solidarity with the February Revolution:

> That this May-Day demonstration convened by Leeds Labour Party and Leeds Trades Council representative of the Labour and Socialist forces in the City, send to the Workers and Soldiers Committee in Russia their warm and whole-hearted congratulations on the magnificent achievement of the Russian people in the long struggle against serfdom, official tyranny and persecution, and in favour of democracy and political liberty. It expresses the strong conviction that the Revolution in Russia and the overthrow of despotic Czarism will be a great liberating force throughout Europe, and will help forward the cause of the peoples who are struggling for political and economic freedom. It is further of opinion that the Revolution will tend in the direction of international solidarity, and will hasten the coming of a peace based not on the dominance of militarists and diplomatists but upon the principles of Nationality, Democracy and Justice.

'It was a glorious day for such a meeting,' reported the *Leeds Weekly Citizen*, 'for the sun shone from a blue sky, and there was no chill in the air, and the day lent itself to the note of hope and optimism which several speakers struck very happily.' Harold Clay, a member of the BSP and chair of Leeds Labour Party, commented on the February Revolution in Russia: 'Nor was the work over yet. They had overthrown Czardom, but the struggles today seemed to be between the militarist section, represented by Miliukoff [Minister of Foreign Affairs in the Provisional Government], and the democratic section, represented by the Workers and Soldiers Committee.'[7] On 13 May 1917, Glasgow held a mass rally with George Lansbury, W.C.

Anderson MP and Robert Smillie among the billed speakers.[8]

It was amid this rising movement and the new feeling of optimism among workers after three years of war that, on 11 May, the newly reformed 'United Socialist Council of the Independent Labour Party and British Socialist Party' called for a national delegate conference to be held in Leeds on Sunday 3 June 1917, its first major initiative.[9] The members of the committee putting out the call included leading Labour Party figures such as J. Ramsay MacDonald, Philip Snowden, George Lansbury, Charles Ammon and William Crawford Anderson, key trade union leaders such as Robert Williams and Robert Smillie, and prominent socialists such as Tom Quelch, Charlotte Despard and Fred Jowett. The appointed secretaries were Albert Inkpin (BSP) and Francis Johnson (ILP).

Albert Inkpin   *Francis Johnson*

The initial circular, entitled 'Follow Russia!', noted:

> The events which have recently taken place in Russia call for a reply on the part of the British Socialist and Labour Movement. It is considered desirable and necessary by the undersigned that a Conference shall be convened of representative organisations to congratulate and encourage our Russian comrades upon the success they have achieved in overthrowing the reactionary forces of that country and establishing real political freedom.

The newly enfranchised Russian democracy are becoming increasingly despondent of the Great Britain which they once considered the home of liberty and progress. Dissatisfaction has, moreover, been manifested against the reactionary forces in this country nominating and selecting individuals ostensibly to represent the Labour and Socialist Movement of Great Britain. In Russia, where the people have assumed control over their own political circumstances, they are repudiating the policy of imperial conquest and annexation, and declare repeatedly in favour of peace without annexations and indemnities. They have, moreover, called upon the common people in all the belligerent countries to throw over their reactionary Governments which are at times in favour of conquest and imperial aggrandisement.

Not only is it the duty of the German and Austro-Hungarian working class to repudiate the dreams of conquest of their rulers, but it is clearly the duty of the working class of Great Britain to repudiate aims and aspirations – dynastic, territorial and capitalist – that were supported by the Russian Czardom, and which have materially influenced the collective aims of the Allies.

We, therefore, feel it our urgent duty to convene a representative conference of Trades Councils, local Labour Parties, Socialist organisations, and women's industrial and political organisations, in order to ascertain and pronounce upon the opinions of the working class of this country regarding the developments which have taken place, and are taking place in Russia. We are, moreover, especially anxious that Trade Union branches and District Councils or Federations of Trade Unions shall be represented at this Conference, and they will receive credentials at their own request.

It is becoming increasingly evident that the forces which brought about war are unable to make peace. Just as the Russian democracy have taken the most significant steps in favour of an international peace, so must the democratic forces in every country strive to emulate their magnificent example. If the Russian people receive no sympathetic response to their call for an international peace from the people of the Allied countries, they may be driven into a separate peace with the Kaiser's reactionary government. It is our duty to work for a complete and real international peace based upon working-class solidarity, and, therefore, calculated to be honourable and enduring.

The Conference will take place in Leeds on Sunday, June 3, and the basis of representation will be one delegate for every 5000 members or part thereof. The delegation fee will be 2s.6d. per delegate. It is hoped that the great Trades Councils and local Labour Parties and all branches of the

21

Independent Labour Party and the British Socialist Party will provide for strong representation, in order to make the Conference as representative and powerful as possible. Those Trade Union branches and District Councils which feel that they are entitled to separate representation may do so on the basis indicated above. Will all secretaries and sympathisers place this matter before their respective organisations at the earliest possible moment? The Conference will take place exactly a week before the Stockholm meeting of the International, at which the international situation will be considered by working-class representatives from all countries. The Leeds Conference will be destined to have a great and far-reaching effect upon the international situation. The plans of the imperialists, militarists, and aggressionists throughout Europe can only be thwarted by concerted action on the part of the working class, now rapidly returning to their adherence to the principles of the International Solidarity of Labour.[10]

The conference was to be carefully structured, the 'rigid rules' referred to in the circular allowed those proposing resolutions to speak for 10 minutes whilst seconders were allotted 5 minutes, and no additional resolutions were to be accepted from the floor.

On 25 May 1917, the Cabinet was informed that 'a large Labour, Socialistic and Democratic Conference' was to be held at Leeds but, despite its 'revolutionary' character, as the conference had been widely publicised, it was thought prudent not to prohibit the gathering.[12] Snowden recalled that 'if there had been any strong popular feeling against the holding of such a Convention it would certainly have organised itself. For weeks before the date of the Convention the Press had been denouncing the Convention and inciting the rowdy elements to opposition.'[13] The fourth resolution, relating to the formation of Workmen's and Soldiers' Councils (along the lines of those in Petrograd), was particularly controversial. The *Morning Post* asserted that the resolution was as 'clearly a violation of the law as inciting to the subversion of Army discipline and the military authorities'.[14] The press hysteria around this resolution was such that even the support of the local Labour Party and Trades Council in Leeds for the Convention was not unanimous and unconditional.[15] In Leeds itself notice of the Convention had first appeared in the *Leeds Mercury* on 12 May, 'No Annexation Conference to be held in Leeds'. Thereafter the local press appeared largely uninterested but when, on 25 May, the *Leeds Weekly Citizen* (linked to local Labour Party) published the resolutions to be

Having initially secured the Albert Hall in Leeds, the United
Socialist Council put out the following call 'to follow Russia'
on 23 May 1917[11]

Great Labour, Socialist *and* Democratic Convention
to hail the Russian Revolution
and to Organise *the* British Democracy

To follow Russia

May 23rd, 1917.

To Trades Councils, Trade Unions, Local Labour Parties, Socialist Parties, Women's Organisations, and Democratic Bodies.

DEAR COMRADES,

The Conference to which we recently invited you is already assured of a **great success.**

It will be one of the greatest Democratic Gatherings ever held in this country. It will be historic. It will begin a new era of democratic power in Great Britain. It will begin to do for this country what the Russian Revolution has accomplished in Russia.

There is little time for preparation. Action must be taken immediately by every Branch and Society desiring to be represented. It seems not unlikely, owing to the rush of applications for delegates' tickets that the Committee may be unable to give facilities for those who delay till the last moment.

The Conference will be held in the **ALBERT HALL, LEEDS,** on **SUNDAY, JUNE 3rd,** commencing at **10.30 a.m.**

We now send you the Resolutions which are to be discussed. Owing to the shortness of time for the preparation for the Conference the proceedings will not be subject to the rigid rules which usually govern Labour and Socialist Congresses. It will be a Democratic Conference to establish Democracy in Great Britain.

Russia has called to us to follow her. You must not refuse to answer that appeal.

Send in your application for Delegates' Cards at once. You are entitled to send one delegate however small your membership may be, but an additional delegate for each 5,000 of your membership above the first 5,000, or part of 5,000.

Applications, accompanied by a fee of 2s. 6d. for each delegate, must be sent to one of the Secretaries as under:

ALBERT INKPIN, Chandos Hall, 21a Maiden Lane, Strand, London, W.C.2
FRANCIS JOHNSON, St. Bride's House, Salisbury Square, London, E.C.4

In the confident hope that your Society will join in this great event,

On behalf of the United Socialist Council,

We remain,

Yours fraternally,

H. ALEXANDER	GEO. LANSBURY
CHAS. G. AMMON	J. RAMSAY MACDONALD
W. C. ANDERSON	TOM QUELCH
C. DESPARD	ROBERT SMILLIE
E. C. FAIRCHILD	PHILIP SNOWDEN
J. FINEBERG	ROBERT WILLIAMS
F. W. JOWETT	

discussed at the Convention, the wider local press coverage became extremely hostile.[16] On 1 June an editorial in the *Leeds Mercury* urged 'Every loyal citizen of Leeds to remember that those behind the conference represent a mere handful of fanatics with a distorted vision and a peculiar twist on their consciences, which happily does not afflict many but a mere handful of perverts like themselves'. In the face of media hysteria, the organising committee struck back and paid for large advertisements for the Convention in the *Daily News*, the *Manchester Guardian*, the *Star* and 'seven or eight provincial papers'.[17] *The Herald* noted just before the event that 'applications for credentials have poured in from all parts of the country', with a thousand expected delegates representing many thousands. 'The Conference will hail the Russian Revolution. It will be the first representative gathering of the British Labour movement to express unqualified approval of what the Socialists of Russia have accomplished.' It noted that in the week leading up to the Conference, Philip Snowden issued an 'interesting manifesto on behalf of the United Socialist Council', declaring that:

> It is not an ordinary Conference at which a few resolutions will be passed after which the delegates will separate and nothing more will be done. The Convention on Sunday is to be the beginning of doing things in this country. The war itself, and all the mismanagement of it, as well as the evident incapacity of the Governments at war to settle the conflagration they have set blazing, call to the democracy of this and all the other belligerent countries to take matters into their own hands, as the people of Russia have already done. That is the only way the war can be brought to an end. It is the only way in which an enduring peace can be established. The settlement of the war by an honourable peace, on the lines set forth by the Russian democratic Government, is the immediate question for the international democracies. But the war when settled will have left industrial and social problems of immense and vital importance, which can only be dealt with properly organised democratic forces. At present British Labour and British democracy is without a policy and without direction. The Convention is intended to provide both, and to begin such vigorous activity in this country as we have never seen in our time. Now is the time to realise the international call, 'Workers of All Lands Unite!'[18]

In the event, as the *Yorkshire Post* reported on 4 June,

> The Convention did not meet at the Albert Hall as originally planned but at nearby Coliseum. The booking for the Albert Hall had been made by Leeds councillor, John Arnott of the ILP. According to DB Foster speaking at the Leeds Labour Party meeting of 31st May, a member of the British Empire League had been despatched from London to Leeds to visit every committee member of the Leeds Institute to persuade them withdraw the booking. The cancellation of the booking was also urged by the local press.

Similar pressure was brought to bear on Leeds hoteliers to cancel room bookings and indeed some delegates already occupying hotel rooms, were asked to leave. The open air demonstration which was scheduled to take place in front of the Town Hall was banned on instructions from the Home Office, but an evening meeting was held in the Coliseum under the chairmanship of Harold Clay, chair of the Leeds Labour Party with speakers including W.C. Anderson and Mrs Despard. Although the day's proceedings in the Coliseum had been orderly, after the evening meeting a number of 'lads' followed the departing delegates to the Midland Station boo-ing and shouting 'Traitors'.[19]

None the less, the Convention was able to take place, as *The Herald* reported:

The Conference convened by the United Socialist Council and designed to hail the Russian Revolution was held in the Coliseum Theatre, Leeds, on Sunday. Although the meeting-place had been changed at the last moment, in consequence of the refusal of the authorities to permit the use of the Albert Hall, the Conference proceeded smoothly, a tribute to the work of the joint-secretaries, Francis Johnson, of the I.L.P. and Albert Inkpin, of the B.S.P., and their colleagues. In spite of Press attempts to work up violent opposition on the part of the townspeople, there were no 'scenes' of any importance. Even the foolish attempt of hotel proprietors to refuse accommodation to delegates was completely overthrown. About 1,200 delegates attended, including 209 from Trades Councils and local Labour Parties, 371 from the Trade Unions, 294 from the I.L.P., 86 from the B.S.P., 16 from other Socialist societies, 54 from women's organisations, and 118 from miscellaneous bodies such as the National Council for Civil Liberties and the Union of Democratic Control. The outstanding incident was the decision to form a Workers' and Soldiers' Council on the lines of the Councils in Russia. An open air demonstration arranged to follow the Conference was prohibited by the authorities, but a large and enthusiastic indoor meeting was held. The organisers had prophesised that the occasion would be historic. It was.[20]

The Coliseum building – one hundred years on from the Leeds Convention

WHAT HAPPENED AT LEEDS

Report Published by the Council
of Workers' & Soldiers'
Delegates

1917
LONDON
4 DUKE STREET
ADELPHI
W.C

Reprint of Convention Report 'What Happened at Leeds'
(reproduced as formatted in original booklet)

THE Leeds Convention of June 3rd was attenaed by 1,150 delegates from democratic bodies. The representation was made up as follows:—

Trades Councils and local Labour Parties	209 delegates
Trade Union Organisations	371 „
Independent Labour Party	294 „
British Socialist Party	88 „
Other Socialist Societies	16 „
Women's Organisations (including Women's Labour League, Women's International League, and Women's Co-operative Guild)	54 .,
Other Organisations (including Adult Schools, Co-operative Societies, Union of Democratic Control, National Council for Civil Liberties, Peace Societies, and May-Day Committees)	118 „

By its fourth resolution the Conference set up a Council of Workers' ana Soldiers' Delegates, and appointed as members of the Central Committee the thirteen conveners of the Conference: H. Alexander, Charles G. Ammon, W. C. Anderson, M.P., C. Despard, E. C. Fairchild, J. Fineberg, F. W. Jowett, M.P., George Lansbury, J. Ramsay Macdonald, M.P., Tom Quelch, Robert Smillie, Philip Snowden, M.P., and Robert Williams. Thirteen members will be added to this number by the votes of district conferences, which will cover the whole country. These district conferences will take place in July.

Joint Secretaries of the Convention: A. Inkpin (B.S.P.), Francis Johnson (I.L.P.)

❧ MESSAGES AND LETTERS

From the RUSSIAN SOLDIERS' AND WORKERS' DEPUTIES

THE friendly Executive of the Soldiers' and Workmen's Deputies sends salutations and fraternal greetings to the Conference of Socialist and Workmen's Organisations at Leeds, and hopes to meet the representatives of the Leeds Conference between July 15 and 30. (*Cheers.*)

The Executive Committee finds Stockholm the most convenient place for the Conference. The agenda has not yet been definitely settled, but will be telegraphed to you later.

From GEORGE LANSBURY

It is a great disappointment to me not to be with you, but here I am on my back—a crock. I send you this message to congratulate you on coming together. You are taking part in a world-wide movement—a movement which may be hindered but can never be stopped. The Russian Revolutionists have not just an academic belief in their principles. They are determined to put them into action—they are putting them into action. It is the uprising of the proletariat. How shall we answer? We, too, must prove that when we talk of Liberty, Equality, Fraternity, we mean exactly what we say. Not liberty for just a few; not equality in this or that section ; not fraternity only in some nations or races ; but Liberty, Equality, and Fraternity the world over. Let us show our Government—our Provisional Government—(*cheers*)—that we have learned one of the lessons they have been trying to teach Russia—the lesson of what the military call "The Unity of the Fronts." Our front also is one—one with our brothers of the proletariat in Russia, in France, in Germany—(*cheers*)—in Austria, in Italy, in the United States—one with all the world's workers, who have been deluded, coerced, exploited by their Governments in this war. (*Cheers.*) Comrades, be strong in the work which you have set yourselves. Remember who you are, representatives of the great mass of the people in this country. I hope the Conference will send Robert Smillie and Robert Williams to Stockholm—(*cheers*)—and let us all send out one unanimous shout for International Solidarity —Solidarity—Solidarity. It is the slogan which will take us forward to a triumphant issue. When they condemn you for wanting peace, when they charge you with treason for being determined to end the war, tell them that it is treason against God, treason against humanity, not to end it—and at once. (*Cheers.*)

From a R.A.M.C. UNIT

We were very glad to see in this morning's *Manchester Guardian* a notice of a Conference to be held at Leeds shortly. We feel it our duty to write to you on the subject, as we think that the holding of such a Conference is a step in the right direction—("Hear, hear")—as the restatement of British war aims, and more especially the opening of negotiations between the belligerents are absolutely necessary. We should very much like to see the establishment of a society on lines similar to those of the Council of Soldiers' and Workmen's in Russia, for we are quite convinced that the great majority of men in the Army are in sympathy with the Russian aims. (*Cheers.*) The difficulty is that the views of the Army and the workers in this country have no medium of expression. This would be remedied by the formation of a body representing the soldiers and workmen. Meantime we assure you of our cordial support, such as it is, and our gratitude for the taking of such steps, which can be the only basis for a lasting and democratic peace. I would place on record the fact that we are all soldiers of two years' service or more, and also late members of the B.E.F.

From CLIFFORD ALLEN

Dear Mr. Smillie,—Three hours ago I received my third sentence of hard labour here—this time for two years. ("Shame.") I go back to prison to-morrow. Before I go may I be allowed to send you a personal message of goodwill, with profound gratitude for the heroic struggle you are making outside, and probably you may convey to the Leeds Convention the greetings of 1,000 Conscientious Objectors at present serving their second, third, or fourth sentences. I thrilled with delight when within the prison it was whispered that the Russian Democracy had at last triumphed, and my hopes became brighter when, upon my return to the military cells, I saw that the Russian Revolution meant international re-birth. I am wearing the khaki in this cell, so that I may consider myself part of the soldier section of your Convention, and perhaps after two sentences of hard labour I am entitled to consider myself a worker. (*Laughter and a voice:* "Let us fetch him out!") I go back to prison to-morrow for two years with renewed courage, which is born of the knowledge that all over the country and the world the spirit of true freedom and service has been re-awakened.

◥ SPEECHES

ROBERT SMILLIE (*Chairman*)

This meeting is the outcome of a series of meetings welcoming the Russian Revolution which have been held in different parts of the country. I think the promoters of the great Albert Hall meeting in London deserve the thanks of the democracy of this country. (*Cheers.*) They seized the psychological moment. Now it has been thought wise to concentrate the enthusiasm that has been evinced in every part of the country in this great central Conference, representative of the democracy and of organised Labour in this country. I don't think it would have been possible to have held meetings such as have been held in London, Manchester, Glasgow, and the other great centres, nor this great representative Conference, had it not been for the Russian Revolution. We in this country had reached the stage at which we were not in a position to call our souls our own. The right to call our bodies our own had gone a considerable time before. If it is a right thing that the Russian people are to be congratulated on securing their freedom, surely it cannot be a wrong thing for Britain to desire freedom also. Now, we have not come here to talk treason. We have come here to talk reason. (*Cheers.*) I am glad to know that practically all opposition has been removed so far as the first three resolutions are concerned. Surely no person in this meeting or in this city or in Great Britain can now afford to refuse to send congratulations to our comrades in Russia. I don't see how there can be any reasonable objection to the demand for a restatement of foreign policy and war aims. As for the third resolution, civil liberty to me is one òf the most important things in the world. Without civil liberty life is not worth living. We haven't civil liberty in this country now. ("Hear, hear.") I come to the last resolution. Our soldiers are inarticulate. They have no organisation to advocate their claims and to call attention to their grievances. Does anyone say there is no need for such an organisation to be set up? Has the treatment of the relatives and dependents of those at the Front been so good up to the present time that nothing further need be done? Has the treatment of the soldiers themselves at the Front, or when they were wounded, or when they were retired from the Army—has it been all that could be desired? There must be a closer link between the civil population and the military population.

We want to endeavour to concentrate the opinion and will of the people in this country on peace. (*Loud cheers.*) I think it is fairly well agreed now that the Central Powers cannot knock out the Allies or the Allies knock the Central Powers out. When peace comes—even if it is forty, fifty, or sixty years hence—it will be peace by negotiation. (*Cheers.*) Is there any use in murdering a few millions more of the sons of the people? ("No.") We want a lasting peace, and a lasting peace cannot and will not be brought about by kings and negotiators. Such a peace can be made only by the common people. (*Cheers.*) I have no desire to see Russia make a separate peace at the present time. But the Russian people are perfectly entitled to tell us that they have stated their aims perfectly clearly. They are entitled to ask us to state our position equally clearly. If we and France and Italy join with America and Russia in denouncing Imperialism and annexation, I believe the German Government would be forced by public opinion in Germany to negotiate on similar terms, or the German people would take the step which has been taken by the Russians. (*Cheers.*)

THE FIRST RESOLUTION
RUSSIA HAIL!

This Conference of Labour, Socialist, and Democratic organisations of Great Britain hails the Russian Revolution. With gratitude and admiration it congratulates the Russian people upon a Revolution which has overthrown a tyranny that resisted the intellectual and social development of Russia, which has removed the standing menace of an aggressive imperialism in Eastern Europe, and which has liberated the people of Russia for the great work of establishing their own political and economic freedom on a firm foundation, and of taking a foremost part in the international movement for working-class emancipation from all forms of political, economic, and imperialist oppression and exploitation.

Moved by J. RAMSAY MACDONALD, M.P.; seconded by Mrs. MONTEFIORE.

J. RAMSAY MACDONALD

I think there will be no minority upon this resolution. It is fashionable in some quarters in this country to say, We congratulate the Russians upon the

Revolution, but in some respects we regret it. (*Laughter.*) But to-day we congratulate the Russians on the Revolution without any reservations whatever. We do it not because the Revolution has happened, but because for years we wanted it to happen. We are glad not because we are compelled to be glad—("Hear, hear"; and *laughter*)—but because it is in accordance with our democratic principles to be glad. The Revolution did not come in a night. ("Hear, hear.") Never has precious harvest been sown with more precious seed. ("Hear, hear.") The best of the women of Russia, the best of the men of Russia, the young women and the young men, laying down their lives that liberty might be advanced in their native land—all that story of oppression, all that long tale of martyrdom, is drawn like a trail of blood across the history of Russia, at last bursting out into a great flood of light and hope, not only for Russia, thank God, but for the whole of the world. (*Cheers.*) Our congratulations are absolutely unstinted and unqualified. ("Hear, hear.") And what has it done for Russia itself? The moment the Revolution came the gates of the prisons were unbarred—(*cheers*)—censorships were abolished, and the light of reason allowed to play upon the problems of the world. Russia for the first time was free to speak, free to think, free to act; and that freedom has sweetened and ennobled the thoughts of mankind. (*Cheers.*)

The old Russian Government was a sink of corruption. It was the most corrupt of all the Governments of Europe. St. Petersburg was the nursery of the very worst forms of diplomacy, the garden where the worst traditions of diplomacy were carefully watered and nurtured. Its policy was bound ultimately to make for war. All was restless, all was untrustworthy, all was unsafe, all was criminal. When this war broke out organised Labour in this country lost the initiative. ("Hear, hear.") It became a mere echo of the old governing classes' opinions. ("Hear, hear.") Now the Russian Revolution has once again given you the chance to take the initiative yourselves. Let us lay down our terms, make our own proclamations, establish our own diplomacy, see to it that we have our own international meetings. Let us say to the Russian democracy, "In the name of everything you hold sacred in politics, in morality, in good government, and in progress, restrain the anarchy in your midst, find a cause for unity, maintain your Revolution, stand by your liberties, put yourselves at the head of the peoples of Europe." (*Cheers.*)

Mrs. MONTEFIORE

I am proud to be able to second this resolution of greeting to our Russian comrades in their successful Revolution against imperialism and against all the evil forces that bound their nation. "Russia is in the act of creating a new world" —I am quoting from a capitalist paper of yesterday, which added that it did not think the moment was propitious for this act of creation. (*Laughter.*) I read yesterday a letter from a young officer in the trenches: "One of the greatest tragedies of the war is to see the idealist laying down his life for a peace that is to be arranged by the materialist." Our soldiers are thinking furiously. Our part is to see that peace is not made by materialists. ("Hear, hear.") This meeting I hold to be a consecration of ourselves. Every resolution on the programme to-day asks for action. The democratic power that can end this war

and bring in peace can also bring in the Co-operative Commonwealth. (*Cheers.*)
Are you prepared to mobilise for the great fight at the end to do away with wage
slavery? (*Cheers.*) You are then from to-day each consecrated and mobilised in
that army. Each one going away can get your five, ten, twenty, one hundred
followers.

*The Chairman said that the Irish comrades present wished to have the words
"and Ireland" inserted after "Great Britain," as hailing the Russian Revolution.
This being agreed to the resolution was carried unanimously.*

⟨ THE SECOND RESOLUTION
FOREIGN POLICY

*This Conference of Labour, Socialist, and Democratic organisations of Great
Britain hails with the greatest satisfaction the declaration of the foreign policy and
the war aims of the Russian Provisional Government, and it shares with them the
firm conviction that the fall of Tsardom and the consolidation of democratic principles in Russia's internal and external policy will create in the democracies of other
nations new aspirations towards a stable peace and the brotherhood of nations. In
that belief we pledge ourselves to work for an agreement with the international democracies for the re-establishment of a general peace which shall not tend towards either
domination by or over any nation, or the seizure of their national possessions, or the
violent usurpation of their territories—a peace without annexations or indemnities
and based on the rights of nations to decide their own affairs; and as a first step
towards this aim we call upon the British Government immediately to announce its
agreement with the declared foreign policy and war aims of the democratic Government of Russia.*

Moved by PHILIP SNOWDEN, M.P.; seconded by E. C. FAIRCHILD.

PHILIP SNOWDEN

The enthusiasm of this great gathering tempts a speaker to forget that this
is something more than a demonstration. It is a convention called for calm and
serious consideration of very important questions, and without detracting from
the importance of other resolutions upon the paper. I venture to submit that
the resolution I now move is one of the gravest urgency and importance. It is
a resolution which asks this Convention to accept the declaration made three
days ago by the congress of Russian soldiers, demanding in the name of the men
in the trenches that every effort should be put forward to bring this bloody war
to an end at the earliest possible moment. For three years this great struggle
has been going on. We were told by a member of the War Cabinet a few days
ago that forty-six millions of the manhood of Europe have already been killed
or wounded, and the only talk we get from our statesmen to-day is about preparations for the continuation of the war even next year and the following year.
("Shame.") For three years we have been appealing to the Government to tell
us their peace terms. The time has now come for us to tell the Government
what *our* peace terms are. (*Cheers.*) The resolution I propose adopts almost the
identical phraseology of the first declaration of the Russian Workmen's and
Soldiers' Council. That declaration was afterwards accepted and embodied in

a note to the Allied Powers by the Provisional Government. It declares that the war must be brought to an end as soon as possible by an international understanding between the democracies, and that the basis of peace should be no annexation and no indemnity, and the right of every nation to dispose of its own destiny. What do the Russians mean by "no annexation"? They have very clearly and very explicitly stated that they mean that no territory which has been conquered during the war shall be retained after the war by the right of that conquest alone. In the debate in the House of Commons both the Under-Secretary for Foreign Affairs and Mr. Asquith accepted the general formula, but placed their own interpretation upon it. Lord Robert Cecil, whilst saying that he agreed that there should be no annexation, and whilst repudiating all Imperialist aims and ambitions on the part of the British Government—(*laughter*)— refused to concede one single word of alteration in the Allied Note which was sent in reply to President Wilson four months ago. Mr. Asquith, while accepting the formula " no annexation," went on to point out four conditions under which annexation would be justified, two of which were the annexation of territory for strategical security and purposes, and the liberation of subject peoples groaning under the tyranny of an alien oppressor. (*Loud laughter.*) Both Mr. Asquith and Lord Robert Cecil, while accepting the formula of "no annexation," demand the annexation of 400,000 square miles of territory held by Germany in Africa before the war. And Lord Robert Cecil justifies it by the condition laid down by Mr. Asquith, that this is not imperialism, but is part of the fulfilment of that diverse mission which has been laid upon the British people to release the oppressed wherever they may be found. (*Laughter and cries of* "Ireland!") In dealing with the question of indemnities, Lord Robert Cecil even added a demand to those in the Allied Note—a possible claim for indemnity on account of shipping losses.

I think we all agree that if a permanent peace is to be established there will have to be readjustment of territory. But the Russian declaration provides for that by giving to all peoples the right to dispose of their own destiny. There you have the method by which you can settle all these questions of Alsace-Lorraine, of Poland, of Austria, and of the Balkans. (*A voice:* "Ireland.") I might now add Egypt and India. No annexation, therefore, means no transfer of any territory against the will of the people concerned. It means that instead of foreign policy being conducted in the secret courts of diplomacy, instead of so-called peace settlements being made by the men who made the war, the peace will be a people's peace.

E. C. FAIRCHILD

At this Convention, the very greatest that we have had in this country since the days of Chartism, we are assembled to place ourselves and the working classes of this country in accord with the working classes of Russia, and we hope eventually with the working classes of all countries in the world. We are here to affirm that the future of the world does no longer depend upon its statesmen but upon the decisions of the working people. Let it be clearly understood that every nation has an equal right with ourselves to a place in the sun. The peace must be on the basis of no annexation and no indemnity. With regard to indemnities, may I say that all the nations involved in this war have a common liability. (*Cheers.*) Who can say who is responsible for the devastation of Poland, where opposing armies have crossed the country? Who can say who should be responsible for the restoration of Serbia? Who can say who has caused the devastation on the Western Front? Furthermore, let me remind you that by the imposition of indemnities you only increase the economic burdens of the working classes, and, on the other side, let us remember always that indemnities are a device of imperialist capitalism in order to further its own process of exploitation. All the nations of the world are composed of men with equal rights, and only on that groundwork, the groundwork of the declaration of our Russian comrades, can the peace that we desire be secured. Only a few days ago, in the Chamber of Deputies, it was said that the peace must be a French peace. A French peace no more commends itself to the workers of the world than does a German peace. (*Loud cheers.*) We must have a people's peace. It is not for the workers of all countries to call upon the Germans to overthrow their Government. We have our business here; your business is with our Government. (*Cheers.*)

W. O'BRIEN

In Ireland you have a small nationality at your doors which is demanding its right to live its own life in its own way. We in Ireland were never humbugged by that chaff about the "rights of small nationalities." I gather, from reading some of the capitalist newspapers, that revolution is popular nowadays. Twelve months ago you had a revolution in Ireland. The papers and the politicians that acclaimed the revolution in Russia did not acclaim the revolution in Ireland, where the leaders were taken out and shot like dogs . . . one of them some of you knew—James Connolly. I appeal for you to help us to obtain the release of the 127 political prisoners who are men, and for the one woman who is also imprisoned. She belongs to the aristocracy of Ireland; but she left her class and her family in order to fight with the working class. The men have one privilege, inasmuch as they can talk to one another for an hour a day. She has no one to talk to; she is alone, and is treated as if she was one of the worst of criminals. I ask you to help to obtain her release. The Russian Council of Workers' and Soldiers' Delegates say they want to hear the voice of every section in every country, but will the voice of Ireland be heard? Will the Government allow it? I think this Conference will do a good deal to help us in getting there.

RODEN BUXTON

A great democratic wave is passing, not only through this country, but through all the countries that are at war. The Russians have led the way, and the wave has overflowed the boundaries of Russia and has penetrated into Germany. The great democratic constitutional movement is making its headway there. Look at the position in Austria where the Parliament has been summoned. The demand for the democratic franchise in Hungary can no longer be resisted. Things are moving. In Italy they are discussing a people's peace. It is coming to the fore in every direction. America is not going to fight for imperialistic aims. (*A voice:* "Question.") It will not do so if we lead the way. There is a tide in the affairs of men which taken at the flood leads on to fortune.

We have to take advantage of that tide to-day. Our opponents represent the ebbing tide, but we represent the rising tide. (*Cheers.*)

At the hour for the lunch adjournment, Mr. TUPPER (Seamen's Union) rose to speak. His reference to "Mr. Chairman and comrades" evoked cries of "Withdraw 'comrades.'" The Chairman, appealing for order, asked the Conference to have some dignity about it. The gallant captain continued:—

Mr. TUPPER

I want to raise the question of the merchant seamen who have lost their lives by being torpedoed whilst bringing food to this country. If there are no indemnities, who will be responsible for reimbursing the widows and orphans of the merchant seamen? (*Cries of* "The shipowners.") I can understand you saying shipowners, but they will not do so. (*Cries of* "Make them.") I want to know whether this country is to be saddled with the cost of keeping the widows and children of men who have been foully murdered while bringing food to this country. (*Further disorder, in which the Chairman again appealed for order.*) I want to say this, that the seamen understand warfare as well as anyone else, and what they are asking is: "What right have the enemy, after they have torpedoed a ship, to shell the men in the open boats. Furthermore, may I ask if this Conference will compel the shipowners to pay? (*Cries of* "Yes.") I have said many times in my life in leading strikes that I would compel the shipowners to do this, that, and the other thing. Have we been able to do it? (*Cries of* "Yes.") I say no.

E. BEVIN

I am here to-day, elected not by an Executive of a Union, but by the General Conference of our Union. I have not been instructed how to vote on any resolution, and therefore I shall regard it as an obvious and imperative duty to try and convert my own Union to what I am voting for here to-day. Now, supposing the resolutions become the policy, we will say of a large majority of the Labour movement in this country, and that it is then forced upon the Government. Where do our fatuous friends of the I.L.P. stand with their Bermondsey resolution? When we have arrived at this policy and have associated ourselves with our Russian friends, and there is no response from Germany, will they join in a vigorous prosecution of the war until Germany *does* respond? Our experience of the German Social Democrats in the past was not altogether a happy one. Then, has any evidence come to this country that the German Social Democrats are prepared to reverse their policy? I am not a pacifist, but I object to the present alignment of forces. (*Applause.*) That is all. I am prepared to fight for the principles that I hold. And what is the taking of my life in comparison with the future emancipation of the people from which I came? ("Hear, hear.") We all know that in the industrial world the capitalists would give us peace to-morrow if we would surrender. But I am not going to surrender. I am not going to be a pacifist in the industrial movement. I believe that even in our own country there will have to be the shedding of blood to attain the freedom we require. It is easy to reel off that the people of Alsace-Lorraine shall have a plebiscite vote. We haven t been told how that plebiscite vote is to be taken. No mention has been made as to whether they are prepared to put the question of Africa to a plebiscite vote of the natives of Africa. No mention has been made as to whether the Crown Colonies are to be given a plebiscite vote as to whether they shall decide their form of Government. No mention has been made as to whether they are prepared with all their forces to advocate what means dismemberment of this Empire in order to give the people the right to decide their own form of government. The platform says that "the tide is on the rise for us." For whom? The professional politicians of the Labour Party. (*Disorder, during which the chairman said, "Your time is up, Mr. Bevin."*)

TOM MANN

I desire to congratulate heartily all responsible for bringing this gathering into existence. I hold that it was absolutely essential in the truest interests of the Labour movement and of the country generally that there should be an expression of opinion given at the present time. I am quite sure from my own knowledge that there has been a vast change in the opinion of organised labour and what has hitherto been presented to the nation as its opinion. However true it might have been, it certainly is not true now. There can be no two opinions as to what Russia is demanding. For my part I don't find a single sentence in the resolution that clashes with any belief I have ever held. Why, we have advocated Internationalism a thousand times ten thousand and every other principle contained in the resolution. And if a man should say that he doubts whether they are prepared to behave justly according to their opportunities towards the little nations—say, like Belgium, Serbia, Roumania, Poland, or other countries—can any sane person question their desire and their deep-seated, whole-souled determination? Let us declare now whether we are in favour of these main principles contained in the Russian manifesto issued in May, 1917, principles very well expressed in this resolution. Let us urge France to do the same thing, but before we cry out to France, let us do it ourselves. (*Cheers.*)

The resolution was carried with two or three dissentients.

◥d THE THIRD RESOLUTION
CIVIL LIBERTIES

This Conference calls upon the Government of Great Britain to place itself in accord with the democracy of Russia by proclaiming its adherence to and determination to carry into immediate effect a charter of liberties establishing complete political rights for all men and women, unrestricted freedom of the Press, freedom of speech, a general amnesty for all political and religious prisoners, full rights of industrial and political association, and the release of labour from all forms of compulsion and restraint.

Moved by C. G. AMMON; seconded by Mrs. DESPARD.

C. G. AMMON

I think it would be well if we refreshed our memories as to what exactly the Russian charter of freedom does and so realise what we have lost. It establishes

37

an immediate amnesty for political and religious offences; it establishes freedom of speech, the Press, Labour organisation and the right to strike. Unless we can take them in defiance of the present Administration, do we enjoy any one of these liberties? Many of the best public-spirited men are lying in prison —men like John Maclean, who is now entering upon the second year of his imprisonment. Will you let him go through a third year? ("No.") We have learned recently that seventy-four British subjects have been interned without trial, without any public examination. Recently, Lord Shaw of Dunfermline has pointed out that it is quite possible under present regulations for a victim to be "regulated" to prison or even to the scaffold. We don't realise it and have not taken it seriously enough. In this war for freedom, freedom is a memory and Labour is enchained. What about the treatment of conscientious objectors? Nearly one thousand absolutist conscientious objectors are in prison, some doing their third, some their fourth terms. They will be kept in prison unless we do what Russia has done. (*Cheers.*) Do you know that at the present time the British Government is running what is known as a propaganda department? That department publishes in neutral and Allied countries literature, magazines, and illustrations purporting to give the public spirit, the war spirit of England! Wait a moment; these same publications *must not circulate in this country*. (*Loud laughter.*) Remember that it was from the blood of their martyrs, from the persecutions, the imprisonments, that the good fruit of the Russian Revolution came; perhaps this, too, is the seed of the revolution in this country. (*Cheers.*)

Mrs. DESPARD

We did not have much liberty before the war, but now, when our young men have been sent to the trenches or to prison, we are allowing all liberties to be taken away. I should like everyone here to-day not only to *feel*, but to go out from this hall with an earnest determination to *act*. I know you do not want very much more talk; you want to get to work. God knows, I am ready for prison. (*Cheers.*) I think it was Ruskin who said: "We shall never have true life, we shall never have true action except from those who are ready to die." I think I feel that spirit in this hall to-day. Let us, in Heaven's name, do something, arrange something, whereby in combination we shall be able to show our power, and make the power of the people tell.

F. W. PETHICK LAWRENCE

We are here as citizens of the world to stave off world-ruin, and the world-ruin that might be coming upon us will be coming because of false ideals. The first false ideal is that nationalism is something different and antagonistic and superior to internationalism; and the second false ideal is materialism—the idea that materials are worth more than life and material power more than moral power. A third false ideal is that autocracy is better than democracy, which is exemplified in all the losses of liberty which we are suffering at the present time —the loss of the liberty of the person, the loss of the liberty of speech, and, perhaps worse than both, the loss of the liberty of knowledge; the action of the censor on the one hand, and the action of secret diplomacy on the other. It is for us to restore true ideals in place of false. It is for us to put internationalism in its proper place above, and not below, nationalism; to put interests in their proper place below, and not above, human beings, the men and women of our country. (*Applause.*)

BERTRAND RUSSELL

I wish to say a few words about the thousand men now in prison in this country because they believe in the brotherhood of men. ("Hear, hear.") I don't wish so much to plead on their behalf with you as to convey to you on their behalf the profound joy that it is to them, the profound help in the very difficult time that they have to go through, to feel that the seed of freedom which they have tried to sow is now bearing fruit. They who had to begin their battle when the world was very dark, now have the knowledge that the world looks no longer so dark as it did, and the hope and new happiness which has come into the lives of all of us, that also is with them in prison. Clifford Allen, whom I saw during his brief liberty the other day, takes back with him into his prison the knowledge that the world is moving. He told the court-martial that he stands for liberty—(*cheers*)—as well as for peace. And we who are outside, who by the accident of a few years have failed to have the privilege of standing beside these men, owe it to them to remember how difficult it is for a man anxious to do what he can for his country and for the world to find himself now within prison walls, powerless, unable to help with his counsel, with his enthusiasm, and with his life—able only to sit still within his prison cell. It is that which they feel most, but they and we must know that they have done much to bring about the new state of opinion in this country and the world. It is by their refusal to serve that they have shown the world that it is possible for the individual to stand in this matter of military service against the whole power of the organised State. That is a very great discovery. It is something which enhances the dignity of men, something which makes every one of us feel freer as we look out upon the world. (*Applause.*)

At this stage Mr. SMILLIE *said he wanted to bring to the memory of the Conference their late comrade* KEIR HARDIE.

The members thereupon rose in a body and stood silent.

❧ THE FOURTH RESOLUTION WORKERS' & SOLDIERS' COUNCILS

The Conference calls upon the constituent bodies at once to establish in every town, urban, and rural district, Councils of Workmen and Soldiers' Delegates for initiating and co-ordinating working-class activity in support of the policy set out in the foregoing resolution, and to work strenuously for a peace made by the peoples of the various countries, and for the complete political and economic emancipation of international labour. Such Councils shall also watch diligently for and resist every encroachment upon industrial and civil liberty; shall give special attention to the position of women employed in industry and generally support the work of the Trade Unions; shall take active steps to stop the exploitation of food and all other neces-

saries of life, and shall concern themselves with questions affecting the pensions of wounded and disabled soldiers and the maintenance grants payable to the dependents of men serving with the Army and Navy; and the making of adequate provision for the training of disabled soldiers and for suitable and remunerative work for the men on their return to civil life. And, further, that the conveners of this Conference be appointed a Provisional Committee, whose duty shall be to assist the formation of local Workmen's and Soldiers' Councils and generally to give effect to the policy determined by this Conference.

Moved by W. C. ANDERSON, M.P.; seconded by ROBERT WILLIAMS.

W. C. ANDERSON, M.P.

I gather from Press reports that this fourth resolution is regarded as the ugly duckling among the resolutions, and therefore I claim for it on that ground your special solicitude and support. ("Hear, hear.") I saw a paragraph the other day in that dear old mid-Victorian journal the *Morning Post*—(*laughter*)—which states that the fourth resolution is the one that really matters, being more than mere rhetoric. "This resolution is clearly," it says, "a violation of the law as inciting to the subversion of Army discipline and military authorities." ("Hear, hear.") "Those who move such a resolution and those who act on it are liable to severe penalties." (*Laughter.*) "It is therefore unthinkable that the Government will wittingly permit such action." Well, I move the resolution without any apology of any kind, and if they want criminals (the speaker made a sweep of his arm towards the packed hall), there is a pretty haul of them in this hall. (*Cheers.*) But I wish to say emphatically that the resolution was not intended to be subversive of military responsibilities. What we do say is that soldiers and workmen alike are men and have the rights of men, and we ask the newspapers to howl until they are black in the face if they so desire. (*Cheers.*) We shall go on with the work to which we have laid our hands. (*Cheers.*) If we are going to have justice for the soldiers, for the wives and the widows and the children of the soldiers, and if we are going to have industrial freedom for the workmen, the workman and the soldier must join hands. (*Cheers.*) Ah, they say, this is revolution. If a revolution be the conquest of political power by an hitherto disinherited class, if revolution be that we are not going to put up in the future with what we have put up with in the past, we are not going to have the shams and the poverty of the past, then the sooner we have revolution in this country the better. (*Cheers.*) The present Prime Minister has told Labour to be "audacious" —after the war. There is surely need for some little measure of audacity now. If you wait until after the war there will be very little to be audacious about. What this resolution really means is that we are going to set up throughout the country an organisation linking together these common interests. We are going to try first of all to bring into closer and more organic touch the democracy of Britain with the democracy of Russia and with the democracy of every other country. We are declaring that the peace must be a peace made by the peoples, born of the peoples, and with the stamp of the peoples upon it; not, as in the past, a peace that was no peace, made by rulers and diplomats working in secret behind closed doors. (*Cheers.*) We are building up, taking the first steps to set up the necessary machinery for dealing with the complete emancipation of international labour. Is there no need for that? ("Yes.") Have our rulers made such a job of Europe to-day that the people need take no hand in working out their own destinies and shaping their own life? We demand the full restitution of civil and industrial liberties; we are asking for a means of taking the food-profiteers by the throat. We are asking for an organisation that is going to strengthen Trade Unionism, that is going to have fewer Trade Unions and more combination among workpeople, that is going to strengthen the power of organised Labour and help in every way to enlarge its power. We are going to have an organisation that will care for the broken soldiers and for all the victims of the war. After the Napoleonic Wars, the Crimean, the South African, the war-scarred veteran, wearing a medal for valour, minus an arm, minus a limb, has begged his bread in the street. ("Shame.") That is already coming upon us, and power to prevent it will come not from our rulers but from the awakened conscience of the workmen and soldiers themselves. Therefore, we set up an organisation, not subversive, not unconstitutional unless the authorities care to make it so; an organisation which is a definite challenge to tyranny wherever tyranny may show itself. I would like to suggest this further, that in addition to what is proposed in the resolution—and I believe this is the view of those who have organised this meeting—that this Conference itself, in addition to the organisers of the Conference, should elect at least thirteen more members from its own body in order to work upon the central organisation. I ask you this afternoon not to discuss too much the mere method by which it will be done. These methods will be fully worked out by the Provisional Council, and instructions will be given as to the best means for building up committees locally. We want Great Britain to be great in the true sense—great in literature, in science, in art, great in its conquests of poverty and of justice, great in fame, great in its love of liberty and in its faith in liberty. I believe the most important step in that direction will be the setting up of the committees on the lines suggested. I hope this great Conference, which surely represents the breaking of the ice, the ice that has bound our national feeling during the past two and a half years—this great Congress will speak with no uncertain sound and will give us a mandate to go forward with the work which, in my opinion, will mean the winning back of our liberties in this country, the building up and betterment of labour, and the world-wide brotherhood of man. (*Cheers.*)

ROBERT WILLIAMS

I second the resolution for what it suggests, and for what it implies. I want to read one significant line, the line apparently that has incurred the wrath of the *Morning Post* that Anderson refers to—that the purpose of this committee is to work "for the complete political and economic emancipation of international labour." I want to accept the resolution in its very fullest implication. The resolution, if it means anything at all, means that which is contained in the oft-used phrase from Socialist platforms: The *dictatorship of the proletariat.* (*Cheers.*) I am glad that the Press, the competent Press, the subtle Press, the sinister Press which represents the proprietary interests of this country, have allowed their case against the first three resolutions to go by default, in order to fix themselves steadfastly to the implication of the fourth. My friend Smillie

41

said we have come here to talk not treason but reason; but I would remind Smillie, if he needs it, that under the Defence of the Realm Regulations reason has become treason. (*Cheers.*) We stand steadfastly by this resolution, and we are not going to weaken it by one jot or tittle. If the governing classes in this country are convinced that you are going to give full and adequate effect to this resolution, they will give effect to resolutions one, two, and three in order to defeat you. You have got the most competent, the most capable governing class of the whole world in this country. (*A voice:* "We have beaten them.") You have not beaten them. They have taken your own leaders from your ranks and used them against you. (*Voices:* "Not Smillie.") After they found that Lord Devonport was unable to deal with the profiteers of this country, they wanted to cover up their slimy tracks by putting Bob Smillie into Grosvenor House. They will make every conceivable sacrifice and concession short of getting off your backs. (*Cheers.*) Mr. Tupper demanded that we should fight for indemnities in order to provide adequate sustenance for the dependents of men who have lost their lives in the mercantile marine. If you want restitution, reparation, and guarantees, in God's name get it from the profiteers of your own country. (*Cheers.*) We want a mandate from you to proceed with this resolution, and if there are many amongst you who have got cold feet about this, slip out before the resolution is put. (*Laughter.*) We want to break the influence of the industrial and political labour "machine"—(*cheers*)—and this Convention is our attempt so to do. To-day hundreds and thousands of miners, engineers, transport workers, railwaymen, and the rest are represented here through their Trade Union lodges. We want these men to go back to their constituents and convince them to use the power that lies in their hands to give or withhold their labour in the place where wealth is produced. Parliament will do nothing for you. Parliament has done nothing for you for the whole period of the war. The workpeople have sacrificed in blood and treasure at all times for their country, and the country is theirs by right of those very sacrifices. They say that you will hamper the production of munitions, that control by the workpeople would mean that our national affairs would be less well managed. Smillie referred to Mr. Lloyd George's indictment of the old gang; but every word of Mr. Lloyd George's indictment of the old gang applies even more pertinently to the new gang. (*Cheers.*) The workpeople have been called upon to make sacrifice after sacrifice; the engineering and highly-skilled occupations have had to dilute and water down their highly-skilled labour; you have been called upon to forego your holidays and work long, tedious hours of overtime. We want to assert our right to the ownership and control of the country. We want to demand the representation of the soldiery, of the millions of organised working people in the Army, which, in the words of Mr. Ben Tillett, contains 95 per cent. of the working classes of this country. We are competent to speak in the name of our own class, and damn the Constitution. (*Loud cheers.*) Had the Russian revolutionaries been disposed to be concerned with the Constitution of Holy Russia the Romanoffs would have been on the throne to-day, and I say to you: Have as little concern for the British Constitution as the Russians you are praising had for the dynasty of the Romanoffs. (*Cheers.*) You have a greater right to speak in the name of our people, civilians and soldiers, than have the gang who are in charge of our political destinies at this moment. It has been said by a German intellectual that the proletariat is the rock upon which the church of the future shall be built. It is the rock upon which the reactionary forces will break themselves. (*Cheers.*) If you are really sincere in sending greetings to Russia, I say to you: "Go thou and do likewise." (*Cheers.*) The need for far-reaching, for revolutionary changes is as great in this country as it was in Russia. The workpeople have assumed the directorate of matters in Russia. "Workers of the world unite. You have nothing to lose but your chains, and you have the world to win." (*Cheers.*)

Mrs. PHILIP SNOWDEN

One of the most poisonous of lies from a perjured Press during the war has been the impression they have endeavoured to convey that the movement which we represent was antagonistic to the soldiers and their interests. It is because we care so much for the men who are compelled to sacrifice their lives, which ought to be lived out under God's sun to a blessed end, that we are seeking their comradeship and support and working for them now. I understand from those who know the Russian language that the word "workmens," in the title of our resolution, is a loose translation of a better Russian word "workers." ("Hear, hear.") I make that point only for this reason—that it was not meant by the use of the word "workmens" to keep off those councils suitable women if elected to them. (*Cheers.*) The Russian Revolution owes as much to women as to men. The Russian revolutionaries are honouring women by placing them upon their councils; they are doing common justice to the women by giving them the vote. Keep up your hearts when this Conference is over, and you have to meet the dismal people who can see no light ahead. Get ahead with the formation of our council, and end the war at the speediest possible moment. (*Loud applause.*)

SYLVIA PANKHURST

I trust you will all support this resolution, because it is an attempt to make a straight cut for the Socialist Commonwealth that we all want to see. I believe that this Provisional Committee will be the Provisional Government, like the Russian Socialist Government, some day; and I am very glad to feel that at last we shall come out of this slough of despond, and that the workers will be united in common action. We have had resolutions which have talked about "encroachments upon liberty," but we have never had real liberty in this country. What we want to do is to extend the bounds of liberty further and further. The revolution in Russia is not only political but also industrial. I hope you are going to see to it that some of the women you choose are those sweated workers and the mothers who live in the hovels and slums. I hope you are not going to leave them out when you form your Committees and your Central Government. (*Cheers.*)

FRED SHAW

As one of the rank and file I support this resolution because of its revolutionary possibilities. The time is ripe for the working classes to take things into their own hands and follow Russia. This war has driven out of the minds of the workers many of the old middle-class ideas about the State. We must go forward and ignore all the coercion that the Capitalist State can bring upon us.

R. C. WALLHEAD

I impress upon you the necessity for the formation of committees of this description in order to see that justice is done, not only to men who may come back from the front, but also to the people who remain at home. I belong to the fatuous I.L.P., a party whose record shines as bright as the record of any political party in the country, and who have done as much to preserve working-class freedom and Trade Union freedom as any Trade Union leaders have done. We had some talk of indemnities this morning. You will pay an indemnity, but it will be an indemnity to the winning class in your own country. I believe that these new committees are necessary, and I believe that from them will spring a new democratic force that will begin to rebuild this country for the people. (*Applause.*)

J. SANDERS

I represent a Union who have just come through a strike and are never happy unless we are in a strike. I do hope that the forming of these committees will not be left to those on the platform alone. We have men and women in the body of this hall who are anxious and willing to take part in this great struggle which has got to come. It is not because we don't want them to have all the praise, but we don't want them to have all the danger. I ask the conveners of this meeting to allow members in the body of this hall to participate in this innovation which is going to have such far-reaching effects.

Mrs. CRESSWELL, from Poplar, voiced the hope of women in the East-End that the working woman would be represented on the Council.

J. TOOLE

I was instructed to support the three previous resolutions. I am very sorry to interfere with the harmony of the meeting, but at the same time it is my duty to point out, as representing a certain section of opinion, that there are already sufficient organisations to do the work which has been outlined—Trades Councils, local Labour Parties, Socialist organisations, and various other organisations. Russia and this country suffer from entirely different sets of circumstances. In Russia the Council of Workmen's and Soldiers' Delegates was only established when the monarchy and autocracy had been overthrown. You will have to be very careful that you put on this committee only men over military age.

W. GALLACHER

This Conference seems to be agreed that the Russian Revolution is definitely settled, but is it? No. The Russian Workers' and Soldiers' Delegates have the biggest fight on, not against the capitalists of Russia, but against the capitalists of other countries who have determined that the Socialists of Russia have to be beaten back. Give your own capitalist class in this country so much to do that it will not have time to attend to it.

NOAH ABLETT

So far we have heard ideas we have heard thousands of times before, and with which we all agree. There is no need for further discussion. But I think there should be before us some sort of programme, some sort of practical suggestion of how we are to set up the Councils.

The resolution was then put to the meeting, and carried amid enthusiasm with only two or three dissentients.

It was agreed that the following reply should be sent to the Russian Workmen and Soldiers' Council:—

"The largest and greatest Convention of Labour, Socialist and democratic bodies held in Great Britain during this generation has to-day endorsed Russia's declaration of foreign policy and war aims, and has pledged itself to work through its newly constituted Workmen's and Soldiers' Council for an immediate democratic peace. The Convention received your telegram of congratulation with gratitude and enthusiasm."

The Convention decided that the country should be divided into thirteen districts, each of which would add a representative to the Provisional Committee.

PRINTED AT THE
PELICAN PRESS
2 GOUGH SQUARE
LONDON E·C FOR
THE COUNCIL IN
JUNE 1917

Dramatis Personae

Janet Douglas and Christian Høgsbjerg

Noah Ablett (1883-1935). A militant socialist with syndicalist views, from 1911 Ablett was a member of the executive of the South Wales Miners' Federation and co-author of *The Miners' Next Step* in 1912. A former student at Ruskin College and an activist in the Plebs League, Ablett was a fine orator who remained a militant socialist to the end of his days. See Joyce Bellamy and John Saville's entry in the *Dictionary of Labour Biography* (*DLB*).

Solly Abrahams (1885-?). Under the name 'Mr. [Abraham] Bezalel', Solly Abrahams, who was born of Russian Jewish parentage and who had been resident in London and Glasgow since 1914 or 1915, addressed the Leeds Convention and made 'an eloquent plea … for the Russians in England who are to be conscribed [conscripted]'. He later reported on the anti-semitic riots which broke out in Leeds after the Convention, on 3 and 4 June 1917.

Henry Alexander. A leading London-based member of the Social Democratic Federation and then the British Socialist Party (which the SDF joined in 1911) and one of the organisers of the Leeds Convention. Resigned with Edwin C. Fairchild from the BSP after it voted to affiliate to the new Communist International in 1919.

Reginald Clifford Allen (Lord Allen of Hurtwood) (1888-1939). From 1911, Allen was an activist in both the Independent Labour Party and the Fabian Society. He was editor of the *Daily Citizen,* an official publication of the Labour Party, from 1913 until its close in 1916. At the outbreak of the First World War, he took a strongly anti-war position and, in late 1914, helped form the No-Conscription Fellowship, becoming its chair. Beginning in 1916, as a conscientious objector he was arrested and imprisoned three times, the last occasion falling just before the Leeds Convention took place. He became a much-admired, heroic figure on the Left for his courage in the face of the British state machine. In 1920 he was the ILP representative with

Richard Wallhead on the joint Labour Party-TUC delegation to Soviet Russia. See John Saville's entry in the *DLB*.

Charles George Ammon (Lord Ammon of Camberwell) (1873-1960). A member of the ILP from its formation in 1893 and a trade unionist in the Fawcett Association, the postal sorters' union, which he eventually led. A pacifist during the First World War, he became parliamentary secretary of the No-Conscription Fellowship and helped organise the Leeds Convention. In 1922, he was elected Labour MP for North Camberwell which he held until 1931. Re-elected an MP in 1935, he accepted a peerage in 1944. See Joyce Bellamy, Bryan Sadler and John Saville's entry in the *DLB*.

William Crawford Anderson (1877-1919). An early activist in the Shop Assistants' Union, Anderson became an ILP activist from 1907, well known for his oratory, and he chaired the ILP from 1910 to 1913. He then worked on the *Daily Citizen*, taking an anti-war position in 1914. In 1915, he was elected as a Labour MP in Sheffield, losing his seat in 1918. In 1919, still a rising star within the Labour Party and seen as a possible future leader, he died suddenly after catching influenza. See David E. Martin's entry in the *DLB*.

Tom Bell (1882-1944). A founder member of the Socialist Labour Party, Bell was a militant shop steward and member of the Clyde Workers Committee who attended the Leeds Convention and then became an important founding member of the Communist Party of Great Britain (CPGB).

Margaret Grace Bondfield (1873-1953). Described by Professor Pamela Fox as 'one of Britain's feistiest shop girls', aged 14 she was apprenticed in a draper's shop and, on moving to London, she joined the National Union of Shop Assistants. Bondfield became an undercover agent for Clementina Black's Women's Industrial Council and, using the pseudonym 'Grace Dare', wrote a series of articles exposing the scandalous conditions experienced by shop girls. By 1898 she was assistant general secretary of her union, and, moving in socialist circles, she helped establish the Women's Labour League in

1906. Neither suffragist nor suffragette, she was chair of the Adult Suffrage Society. A close friend of Ramsay Macdonald and his wife, Bondfield spoke at the ILP's Trafalgar Square Rally in August 1914, and served on the Standing Orders Committee of the Leeds Convention. Bondfield's career is littered with 'firsts': she was the first woman delegate to the annual conference of the TUC in 1899, the first woman to chair its annual conference, and, famously, she became the first woman cabinet minister. She was elected Labour MP from 1923 to 1924 (Northampton) and, between 1926 and 1931, she was MP for Wallsend. In 1920 she was a member of the TUC-Labour Party Mission to Russia where she met Lenin and gave cautious support to the Bolshevik government. See Marion Kozak Miliband's *DLB* entry.

Ernest Bevin (1881-1951). A leading member of the Dockers' Union, in 1922 Bevin helped form the Transport and General Workers' Union of which he became general secretary. In 1940 he served as Minister of Labour in Churchill's wartime cabinet and was later Labour Foreign Secretary.

Harold Clay (1886-1961). Born in Leeds, Clay had founded the Leeds Tenants Defence League in 1914, chaired Leeds Labour Party as a BSP member in 1917 (and would chair the evening rally of the Leeds Convention). Clay would go on to become a leading trade unionist in what became the Transport and General Workers' Union and President of the Workers' Educational Association.

James Connolly (1868-1916). A leading activist in the struggle for Irish liberation, in 1916 Connolly was executed by the British for his part in the Easter Rising.

A.J. Cook (1883-1931). Arthur James Cook became a socialist in the ILP as a young miner in Merthyr Tydfil, first coming to prominence in the Cambrian Coal Dispute in 1910. Cook opposed the First World War and attended the Leeds Convention as a delegate of Porth Trades Council. In March 1918 Cook was arrested and charged with sedition under the Defence of the Realm Act, and was sentenced to three months' imprisonment. In 1924 he was elected general secretary of the

Miners' Federation of Great Britain (MFGB), and in this position worked closely with the CPGB for a period.

Nellie Cressall (1882-1973). A laundry worker in the East End, Annie Cressall joined the ILP in 1907 and in 1913 was a member of Sylvia Pankhurst's East London Federation of Suffragettes. Elected a Labour Councillor in Poplar in 1919, she became one of the Poplar Rate Rebels and was imprisoned in Holloway. She remained active in the Labour Party for the rest of her life and was mayor of Poplar in 1943-4.

Charlotte Despard (1844-1939). A friend of Eleanor Marx and delegate to the Second International, Charlotte Despard was a supporter of the SDF and later the ILP. In 1906 she joined the Women's Social and Political Union (WSPU) and was imprisoned twice. Later, following disagreements about the way the suffragette movement was organised, she left to found the Women's Freedom League. In 1918, she was one of the first women to stand as a candidate at the General Election on a Labour Party ticket. From 1921 she devoted herself to Irish freedom and Irish socialism.

Edwin Charles Fairchild (1874–1955). A leading London-based member of the Social Democratic Federation and then the British Socialist Party, Fairchild took an anti-war position in 1914, becoming a conscientious objector, and became chair of the BSP in 1916. Resigned with Henry Alexander from the BSP after it voted to affiliate to the new Communist International in 1919.

Joseph Fineberg (1886–1957). Born in Poland. After moving to London, Fineberg became active in the Jewish Social Democratic Organisation, a section of the British Socialist Party based in the East End. In 1918 he moved to Soviet Russia, and attended the founding congress of the Communist International in 1919. He became a prominent translator for the Communist International, producing English translations of works by Alexander Bogdanov, Nikolay Dobrolyubov, Ilya Ehrenburg, Vladimir Lenin, Boris Polevoy, Leo Tolstoy and others.

William Gallacher (1881-1965). Born into poverty in Scotland, the son of an Irish father and Scottish mother, he became a socialist activist as a young engineer. In 1915 he became chair of the militant Clyde Workers' Committee, and in 1916 was twice imprisoned for his principled anti-war stance. He attended the Second Congress of the Communist International in August 1921, and on his return became a leading member of the newly formed Communist Party of Great Britain. He became Communist MP for West Fife in 1935, which he held until losing to Labour in 1950.

Albert Inkpin (1884-1944). As a trade unionist in the National Union of Clerks, Inkpin joined the Social Democratic Federation in 1906. As first a leading member of the SDF and then the British Socialist Party (which the SDF joined in 1911), Inkpin was elected general secretary of the BSP in 1913 and then took a principled anti-war stance in 1914. One of the joint secretaries of the Leeds Convention in 1917, Inkpin would later help found the Communist Party of Great Britain in 1920, becoming its first general secretary. Regularly imprisoned during the 1920s for his political activity, in 1921 he had visited Soviet Russia to attend the Third Congress of the Communist International in Moscow.

Francis Johnson (1878-1970). A leading member of Finsbury Independent Labour Party from 1899, Johnson became ILP general secretary in 1904, a post he held until 1924 when he moved to financial secretary. Johnson was (with Inkpin) joint secretary of the Leeds Convention.

Frederick William Jowett (1864-1944). Born in Bradford, Fred Jowett worked in the mills from the age of eight years old. In 1886, he joined the short-lived Socialist League of William Morris and, in 1892, he was elected councillor for Manningham, the first elected Socialist on the council. In 1906 he was elected as an ILP MP for Bradford West and took an anti-war position in 1914. He was chosen as a delegate from the Leeds Convention to visit Petrograd in 1917, but this initiative was blocked by Edward Tupper of the Seamen's Union. Jowett lost his seat in 1918, but was returned for Bradford East in 1922, becoming a cabinet minister, First Commissioner of Works in MacDonald's Government of 1924. Losing his seat that year, he was re-elected again from 1929 to 1931, and remained with the ILP when it disaffiliated from Labour in 1932. See Fenner Brockway's biography, *Socialism over Sixty Years: The Life of Jowett of Bradford* (1946) and David E. Martin and John Saville's entry in the *DLB*.

George Lansbury (1859-1940). After a spell in his youth as a radical Liberal, from 1889 Lansbury became a member of the Gasworkers' Union, the Social Democratic Federation, then the ILP and, after its formation, the Labour Party. He first made his name on the Board of Guardians and then the Poplar Borough Council, formed in 1900. In December 1910, Lansbury was elected MP for Bow and Bromley but resigned his seat in 1912 in solidarity with the suffragettes and instead, in 1913, became editor of the newly formed *Daily Herald,* a socialist paper aimed at trade unionists. Though too ill to attend the Leeds Convention, under Lansbury's editorship *The Herald* helped build and organise the event. In 1921, Lansbury led the Labour Party's Poplar Borough Council rebellion and, in 1922, he was re-elected to parliament. Leader of the Labour Party 1931-35. See Margaret Cole's entry in the *DLB*.

Arnold Lupton (1846-1930). Described as 'the stormy petrel' of the Leeds Lupton family, Lupton was a mining engineer by profession who, from the early 1880s until 1905, taught at the University of Leeds. Supporting the Boers in the Boer War, he told an audience of Castleford miners that the war was being fought for the benefit of the South African mine owners. Lupton was the Liberal MP for Sleaford between 1906 and 1910. Although not an active pacifist at the beginning of the First World War, Lupton considered the introduction of conscription in 1916 an anathema, and he was fined under the Defence of the Realm Act for publishing a pamphlet, *What Are We Fighting For?* According to the *Leeds Mercury* (5 June 1917) he attended the Leeds Convention. Undaunted, he continued to write and circulate anti-war literature and, in 1918, was imprisoned for six months for publishing 'literature of a seditious character'.

James Ramsay MacDonald, (1866-1937). Born into a family of Scottish farmworkers, MacDonald joined the London socialist movement in the late 1880s. By 1900 he was a leading figure in the ILP and was elected secretary of the Labour Representation Committee in 1900. In 1906 he was elected as a Labour MP for Leicester, and served as chair of the Parliamentary Labour Party from 1911 to 1914, until his opposition stance on the war forced him to resign. A founding member of the Union of Democratic Control, he worked alongside the wider Left at events such as the Leeds Convention. In 1918, he lost his seat at Leicester. He opposed the ILP affiliating to the Communist International. In 1922, he was elected MP for Aberavon, and once again became chair of the Parliamentary Labour Party. In 1924 he became Labour's first prime minister in the short-lived minority Labour government and, in 1929, was Prime Minister in the second minority Labour government. In 1931, his proposed cut in unemployment benefits despite TUC opposition led to cabinet resignations, but MacDonald remained Prime Minister in a new 'National' Government of Conservatives, Liberals and fifteen Labour members including Philip Snowden. When this government was returned with a massive majority in 1931, MacDonald (now expelled from the Labour Party) remained as Prime Minister until 1935, when he was succeeded by Stanley Baldwin. See Charles Loch Mowat's entry in the *DLB*.

Arthur MacManus (1889-1927). A member of the Socialist Labour Party and, like Gallacher, a delegate from the militant Clyde Workers Committee to the Leeds Convention. He became a founder member of the CPGB and its first chairman, and was also a leading official in the Communist International. His ashes were interred in the Kremlin.

Lady Constance Malleson (1895-1975). The daughter of Hugh Annesley, 5th Earl Annesley, an actress and writer, romantically attached to Bertrand Russell. Drawn together by their shared pacifism, the couple first met in 1916 when Clifford Allen was arrested.

Tom Mann (1856-1941). Born in Coventry, Mann joined the Social Democratic Federation while a young engineer in the mid-1880s. He made his name as one of the leaders of 'new unionism' alongside Ben Tillett in the London Dock Strike in 1889. In 1894 he became general secretary of the newly formed Independent Labour Party. A leading trade unionist who was deported from many European countries for his organising work, he was first President of the International Transport Workers' Federation. After a spell in Australia, he returned to Britain to help lead the Liverpool General Transport Strike and took a militant anti-war stance, writing the famously seditious 'Open Letter to British Soldiers' [*Don't Shoot*]. A member of the British Socialist Party from 1917 onwards, he later helped form the Communist Party of Great Britain and became chair of the National Minority Movement during the 1920s. A unit of the International Brigade which went from Britain to fight in the Spanish Civil War was named in his honour, the Tom Mann Centuria. After his passing in 1941, Mann was buried in Lawnswood Cemetery in Leeds.

Alf Mattison (1868-1944). Born in Hunslet, Mattison – a veteran socialist, trade unionist and lifelong member of the ILP - was one of three Leeds delegates (the others were Bertha Quinn and David Blythe Foster, a founding member of Leeds Tolstoyan Brotherhood Workshop) present at the Leeds Convention. Mattison was also an archivist and historian of the local labour movement in Leeds, and one of his notebooks among his papers in the Brotherton Library records the following about the Leeds Convention: 'I just dropped in as Ramsay MacDonald was speaking. The place was packed and the atmosphere charged with the greatest enthusiasm. I went to the evening meeting. It was a gigantic affair – packed in every part – there would be close on 3,000 of an audience'.

Dora Montefiore (1851-1933). On learning that she did not have automatic rights of guardianship for her children after her husband's death in 1893, Dora Montefiore became an activist in the women's movement and a member of the National Union of Women's Suffrage Societies (NUWSS) and, between 1905 and 1906, was active in the Women's Social and Political Union (WSPU). From the end of the 19th century she was also active in the ILP and SDF. Her attendances at European conferences led to close friendships with Marxist/feminists such as Clara Zetkin and Alexandra Kollontai. During the First World War she joined the British Socialist Party and was one of their delegates to the founding convention of the Communist Party of Great Britain.

J.T. Murphy (1888-1965). Born in Manchester, John Thomas (J.T.) Murphy became a leading trade union militant in the engineering industry during the First World War, a member of the Sheffield Workers' Committee, and a syndicalist influenced by Tom Mann and James Connolly. He attended the Leeds Convention and, in 1917, was elected to the national leadership of the Workers' Committees and Shop Stewards' Movement and joined the Socialist Labour Party. In 1919, Murphy travelled to Moscow as part of the British delegation to the Second Congress of the Comintern, and now became a founding member of the CPGB and a leading official of the Communist International until his resignation in 1932. His memories of the Leeds Convention are published in *Labour's Big Three: A Biographical Study of Clement Attlee, Herbert Morrison and Ernest Bevin* (London: Bodley Head, 1948).

William X. O'Brien (1881-1968). In the 1890s, O'Brien became a leading member of the Irish Socialist Republican Party in Dublin, and a comrade of James Connolly. An active leading member of the Irish Transport and General Workers' Union, O'Brien played an important role in the Dublin Lockout of 1913. Interned during the First World War for his anti-war stance, with the formation of the Irish Free State O'Brien was elected a TD several times, initially for Dublin South in 1922. In 1930 he tried (unsuccessfully) to have the Irish Free State grant political asylum to the exiled Leon Trotsky.

Sylvia Pankhurst (1882-1960). Sylvia Pankhurst was the second daughter of Richard and Emmeline Pankhurst, who became a very close friend of Keir Hardie. Like her mother and sister, Sylvia was imprisoned on a number of occasions but retained her commitment to socialism. Disillusioned by the arson campaign, she broke with the WSPU in 1913, forming the East London Federation of Suffragettes which combined socialism with the demand for women's suffrage. Welcoming the Russian Revolutions, she visited Russia in 1920, where she met and argued with Lenin! The pro-communist stance of her paper, *The Worker's Dreadnought,* led to a five-month imprisonment on grounds of sedition in 1921. For a short period she was a member of the Communist Party but was expelled when she refused to allow *The Dreadnought* to be controlled by the Party's executive.

George Peet (1883-1967). A member of the BSP and a leading militant shop steward in Manchester who attended the Leeds Convention and later helped form the CPGB.

Emmeline Pethick-Lawrence (Baroness Pethick-Lawrence) (1867-1954). Shocked by the poverty she saw in London whilst undertaking voluntary work, Emmeline Pethick, as she was then, became a socialist and joined the ILP. Introduced by Keir Hardie to Emmeline Pankhurst and Annie Kenney, she agreed to act as treasurer for the WSPU. A brilliant fund-raiser with a flair for publicity, not only did the Pethick-Lawrences' home serve as the WSPU office but, in 1907, she and her husband founded the publication *Votes for Women*. Despite several terms of imprisonment, and their much-needed organisational skills, the Pethick-Lawrences were ousted from the WSPU in 1912 for arguing that its window-smashing strategy was likely to jeopardise mass support. Working with the Women's Freedom League, Emmeline was one of three British women able to attend the Women's Peace Congress in The Hague in 1915. After the First World War she devoted herself to working for world peace and was active in the birth control movement.

Frederick William Pethick-Lawrence (1st Baron Pethick-Lawrence) (1871-1961). After becoming a socialist and marrying Emmeline Pethick, Pethick-Lawrence was imprisoned in 1912 for his activity in support of the suffragettes. After 1914, he helped form the Union of Democratic Control and became a notable conscientious objector, standing as a Peace candidate in April 1917 in the South Aberdeen by-election. In 1923 he was elected Labour MP for Leicester West, serving as Financial Secretary to the Treasury under Snowden in the second Labour Government, but lost his seat in 1931. Returning to parliament as MP for Edinburgh East in 1935, Pethick-Lawrence was leader of the opposition to the Coalition Government from 1942. In 1945 he became a peer, before a short spell as Secretary of State for India and Burma, from 1945 to 1947 in the run-up to independence.

Tom Quelch (1886-1954). The son of the early British Marxist Harry Quelch, Tom followed his father into the Social Democratic Federation.

After joining the British Socialist Party, he took a militant anti-war position and was one of the organisers of the Leeds Convention. In 1920, Quelch was delegated to attend the Second Congress of the Communist International and also attended the Baku Congress of the Peoples of the East. He met Lenin, and was elected to the Executive Committee of the Communist International and to the leadership of the Communist Party of Great Britain. From the mid-1920s he worked for the Union of Construction, Allied Trades and Technicians, and a few years before his death resigned from the CPGB.

Charles Roden Buxton (1875-1942). The third son of Sir Thomas Fowell Buxton, third baronet and Lady Victora Noel, Charles was born into a life of great privilege. Becoming a Liberal, Buxton was elected MP in 1910 and worked to set up the Union of Democratic Control after the outbreak of the First World War. An early member of the 1917 Club, he joined the ILP in 1917 but voted against the resolution to set up Workers' Councils at the Leeds Convention. In 1920, as a leading ILP member he was joint secretary of the Labour-TUC delegation to Soviet Russia, writing up his experiences of staying with a peasant in a book entitled *In a Russian Village* (1922). That year he was elected MP for Accrington, and then again as Labour MP for Elland from 1929 to 1931. In 1930 he left the ILP and attempted to secure peace in Europe amid the rising threat of fascism. See Joyce Bellamy and Margaret Espinasse's entry in the *DLB*.

Bertrand Arthur William Russell, 3rd Earl Russell (1872-1970). Born into a famous aristocratic dynasty, Russell was a notable radical, philosopher and thinker. In 1916 he was dismissed from his post at Trinity College, Cambridge, for his anti-war stance, and in 1918 he was imprisoned for six months for writing that US soldiers would be used as strike breakers in Britain. In 1920, Russell travelled to Soviet Russia with the Labour-TUC delegation, meeting Lenin, Trotsky and Gorky. Whilst there, he was struck by the suffering, famine and undemocratic concentration of State power, recounting his experiences in his book, *The Practice and Theory of Bolshevism*. In 1950, Russell received the Nobel Prize in Literature 'in recognition of his varied and significant writings in which he champions humanitarian ideals and freedom of thought'. During the 1950s and 1960s he campaigned continuously for nuclear disarmament, against the Vietnam War, and against imperialism.

J. Sanders. A member of the London and Provincial Union of Licensed Vehicle Workers (before 1913 the London Cab Drivers' Trade Union), a militant trade union.

Fred Shaw (1881-1951). Born in Lindley near Huddersfield, Shaw became a socialist and, by 1903, was propaganda secretary for Lindley Labour Representation Committee. In 1905, he helped form a Huddersfield branch of the Socialist Labour Party and by 1912, alongside his trade union work in the engineering union, he was a leading member of the British Socialist Party on its anti-war wing. In 1919, Shaw was elected president of Huddersfield Trades Council and, in 1920, he was elected to the first national executive of the Communist Party of Great Britain. He also served on the national committee of the 'Hands off Russia' movement. He was blacklisted and victimised for his militant trade union activities. Shaw left the CPGB in 1923 and joined the Labour Party, becoming Yorkshire organiser of the National Council of Labour Colleges. See John Saville's entry in the *DLB*.

Robert Smillie (1857-1940). Robert Smillie was a central figure in Scottish mining trade unionism who helped form the Scottish TUC. A member of the ILP since its formation in 1893, Smillie helped secure the affiliation of the Miners' Federation of Great Britain (MFGB) to the Labour Party in 1908 and became the first socialist president of the Federation in 1912, the year of the great national miners' strike which lasted six weeks. In 1915 he oversaw the creation of the 'Triple Alliance' between the miners, the National Transport Workers' Federation and the railwaymen, becoming chair. Smillie's popularity was evident at the Leeds Convention, which he chaired. In 1923 he was elected Labour MP for Morpeth, but then suffered a decline in health. See Joyce Bellamy and John Saville's entry in the *DLB*.

Philip Snowden, 1st Viscount Snowden (1864-1937). Born the son of a weaver in Cowling in the West Riding, Philip Snowden joined the

ILP in Keighley, and, after moving to Leeds in 1902, became national ILP chair from 1903 to 1906. That year he was elected Labour MP for Blackburn, and was a key organiser of the Leeds Convention in 1917. He lost his seat amid the pro-war sentiment of 1918. In 1922, he was elected Labour MP for Colne Valley and, in 1924, became Labour's first ever Chancellor of the Exchequer in MacDonald's government. In 1927 he left the ILP and, from 1929 to 1931, again became Chancellor during the austerity of the Great Depression. He did not stand for re-election in 1931, and that year was raised to the peerage as Viscount Snowden of Ickornshaw in the West Riding of the County of York.

Ethel Snowden, (née Annakin), Viscountess Snowden (1881-1951). A popular public speaker on the behalf of the ILP, Edith married Philip Snowden in 1905 (Isabella Ford was a witness at the wedding). After 1906 she was increasingly active in the women's suffrage movement on behalf of the NUWSS. At the end of the War she was elected to the National Executive Committee of the Labour Party and, in 1920, was a member of the TUC-Labour Party delegation to Russia, afterwards publishing a somewhat critical account, *Through Bolshevik Russia.*

Ben Tillett (1860-1943). Trade union leader and Labour MP. Ben Tillett made his name as a national figure in the Labour Movement as leader of the 100,000 strong London Dock Strike of 1889 and champion of the 'New Unionism'. In the aftermath he became general secretary of the new Dock, Wharf, Riverside and General Labourers' Union of Great Britain and Ireland. Tillett contested Bradford for the ILP during the 1890s but, by 1908, was disillusioned enough by attempts at parliamentary socialism to write a pamphlet entitled *Is the Parliamentary Labour Party a Failure?* In 1914, Tillett gave active support to the First World War. He attended the Leeds Convention but wasn't invited to speak. Subsequently, he accused the Convention of being unrepresentative, cynical, hijacked by the middle class and pro-German: 'in the midst of this bloody Armageddon, it has been merely a stage army of fiddling Neros unconscious of its cant'. In 1917, standing on a pro-war platform, Tillett became MP in North Salford, a seat he held until 1924, and he was returned again from 1929 to 1931.

Tillett was a member of the TUC delegation to Soviet Russia in 1924. See John Saville and A.J. Topham's entry in the *DLB*.

Joseph Toole (1887-1945). Joe Toole was born in working class Salford and became interested in the local SDF and socialist politics in Manchester, where he moved in 1908. Toole supported the First World War, but he was also involved for a period with the ILP, appearing as Gorton's ILP delegate in 1916. In 1923 he became Labour MP for South Salford but, after losing his seat in 1924, Toole threw himself into local government work, becoming a local Labour councillor in Manchester, leading the Labour group in the 1930s, and ending up as Lord Mayor in 1936. In 1929 he regained the South Salford seat but lost it in 1931, like many other Labour MPs. See David Howell's entry in the *DLB*.

Edward Tupper (1871-1942). Tupper was a trade unionist active in the National Sailors' and Firemen's Union (later the National Union of Seamen), and particularly active in the 1911 strike in Cardiff. Took a pro-war stance in 1914 on the grounds that the enemy of British merchant seafarers were no longer their employers but German sailors trying to sink British shipping. In 1938 wrote his autobiography, *Seamen's Torch - The Life Story of Captain Edward Tupper*, National Union of Seamen, which includes a discussion of his intervention at the Leeds Convention. In the immediate aftermath of the Convention, Tupper organised among seafarers to block MacDonald, Jowett and Fairchild attending a proposed peace conference in Stockholm in 1917 and then visiting revolutionary Petrograd that year.

Richard [Christopher] Collingham Wallhead (1869-1934). Born in Islington, Wallhead became a socialist during the 1890s, becoming a leading ILP member from the 1900s. He took an anti-war position in 1914 and a few months after the Leeds Convention was arrested under the Defence of the Realm Act for anti-war activity and briefly imprisoned. In 1922 he became the MP for Merthyr, formerly the seat of Keir Hardie, which he held until his death. He visited Soviet Russia in 1920 as an unofficial ILP part of the official Labour-TUC delegation with Clifford Allen, and took an active part in the 'Hands Off Russia' committee (later the Anglo-Russian Parliamentary Committee), though he retained political reservations about Communism and the Communist International. In 1933, he resigned from the ILP after disaffiliation to take the Labour whip. See John Saville's entry in the *DLB*.

Robert Williams (1881-1936). Born in Swansea, Williams began his working life as a coal trimmer at the docks. He was active in socialist politics, becoming a local councillor, and joined the National Amalgamated Labourers' Union at the age of 16, eventually becoming its president. In 1912, Williams was elected as the first secretary of the National Transport Workers' Federation. He opposed the First World War, and was a leading member of the Union of Democratic Control. He visited Soviet Russia in 1920 as part of the TUC-Labour delegation, and was briefly a member of the new CPGB.

Selected Newspaper Reports

Soldiers and Workmen: Establishment of Councils Like Russian. Demand for Statement of Peace Terms: Report on 'Socialist Convention On The War'
Manchester Guardian, 4 June 1917, 'From our Special Correspondent,' p.5.[21]

Leeds, Sunday night

The Labour, Socialist, and Democratic Convention to hail the Russian revolution and organise a British democracy, was held in Leeds today. The meetings were to have taken place in the Albert Hall, as stated in the columns yesterday, but the engagement was broken off by the owners. The Coliseum, however, a larger building with accommodation for about 3,500 persons, was placed at the service of the Convention after the Watch Committee had intimated its readiness to extend the six days' licence attached to the building.

In this the Watch Committee showed more tolerance than owners of most of the large hotels in the city, who apparently had agreed among themselves not to give accommodation to the delegates. Many of the delegates had 'booked' in advance at hotels where, on other occasions, they had been personally welcomed, but in every case, as far as I have been able to ascertain, such bookings were cancelled upon an affirmative answer being given to the question; 'Are you attending the Labour Convention?' As the private accommodation found by local Socialists was far from adequate in such an emergency, 200 or 300 were provided for by a lodging bureau opened by the Socialists of Bradford, and a considerable number had to be billeted in improvised dormitories at the great hall of the Engineers' Club.

The Convention was presided over by Mr. Robert Smillie, president of the Miners' Federation, who was supported on the platform by many of the well-known leaders of the Independent Labour Party and the [British] Socialist Party, and by Mr. Roden Buxton and Mrs. Despard. Mr. Tom Mann, Mr. Bertrand Russell, and Miss Sylvia Pankhurst sat among the general body of delegates, who numbered nearly 1,200, and represented trades councils and unions, local Labour and Socialist parties, women's organisations, and various democratic bodies.

On the whole the conference was of an orderly character. A 'breeze,' started by a decision of the Standing Orders Committee to accept certain amendments and reject others - which position was overthrown by the conference determining to confine itself to the resolutions on the agenda, - developed into a storm later on, when Mr. Tupper protested against consideration not having been given to the amendment sent in by his union, and demanded to know, in the event of no indemnities being given, who would recompense the widows and orphans of merchant seamen who had lost their lives while bringing food to the country. At this time the hour for adjournment had passed, and after about ten minutes of excitement, in which an appeal was made to the conference 'to have some dignity;' the Chairman adjourned the meeting.

Among a number of messages read was one from the Executive Committee of the Workmen's and Soldiers' delegates in Petrograd, sending fraternal greetings, and expressing the hope of meeting representatives from the Convention between July 15 and 30, and mentioning Stockholm as the most convenient meeting place.

Six soldiers at Blackpool wrote saying they would like to see 'the establishment of a society on lines similar to those of the Council of Workmen and Soldiers in Russia, for we are quite convinced that the great majority of men in the army are in sympathy with Russian aims.'

The Speeches

The Chairman, in opening the conference, said that but for the Russian revolution he did not think it would have been possible for the convention to have been held. We in this country were gradually reaching the position in which we could not call our souls our own. The right to call our bodies our own went a considerable time ago. It was strange indeed that the light should have come from the down-trodden people of Russia. If it was right that the Russian people should be congratulated on securing freedom, surely it could not be wrong for Britain to desire freedom also.

After remarking, with respect to the attempts to prevent the meeting by mob law, 'we have not come here to talk treason; we have come here to talk reason,' Mr. Smillie contended that there was real need for linking together the civil and military populations of this country by

63

means of an organisation such as the Council of Workmen's and Soldiers' Delegates in Russia. At the present time, he said, our soldiers were inarticulate. They had no organisation, no right to have an organisation, to defend their claims and to call attention to their grievances.

It was pretty well agreed now, he continued, that peace could not be brought about by what was called the 'knock-out' blow. (Cheers) There was no doubt that when peace did come it would be peace by negotiation. (Renewed cheers.) Was there any use, therefore, in murdering a few million more of our sons? He had no desire to see Russia enter into a separate peace with Germany. (Cheers.) That would be a calamity not only to Russia itself, but to the democratic peoples of the world. But he thought the Russian people were entitled to say they were ready and anxious to make peace and to ask us to state our position. If we and our other allies had the courage to do so – and ultimately we should have to do it – and if, instead of aiming at Imperialism and spread-eagleism, we aimed at giving liberty to the peoples of Europe to govern themselves in their own way, he believed the German Government would be forced by public opinion in Germany to negotiate on moral terms, or the German people would take the steps taken by Russia.

The first resolution congratulated the Russian people upon their revolution. It was moved by Mr. Ramsay MacDonald, M.P., seconded by Mrs. Montefiore (British Socialist Party), and carried without discussion.

Mr. Macdonald, M.P., said that when the war broke out organised labour in this country, owing to a great lack of oversight and political intelligence, lost the initiative; instead of seeing that it took the initiative into its own hands and did not become a mere echo of the opinions of the governing classes. Those classes were never yet able to make anything but a patched-up peace or a military truce, and had never yet done anything but extend the bounds of militarism every time that militarism proved itself a failure. The Russian revolution had given them chance to take hold again of the initiative, and while the war was on was their chance. Let them make their own proclamations, establish their own diplomacy and see to it that they had their own international meetings. The call of the Russian democracy had made it impossible for any Government to deny the right of the people to meet together and make up their minds as to what they wanted and ask the Government to carry out their mandate.

Peace Terms

Mr. Philip Snowden, M.P., moved a resolution in favour of 'peace without annexation or indemnities and based on the rights of nations to decide their own affairs,' and calling upon the British Government 'immediately to announce its agreement with the declared foreign policy and war aims of the democratic Government of Russia.' They had been told, he said, that millions of the manhood of Europe had already been killed or maimed, yet the only talk of statesmen today was about preparations for the continuance of the war into next year or the following year. Their only concern seemed to be to get more men to feed the cannons' mouth.

'For three years,' he continued, 'we have been appealing to the Government to state its peace terms. The time has come for us to tell the Government what our peace terms are.' (Cheers.) Commenting on the debate in the House of Commons and the speeches of Lord Robert Cecil and Mr. Asquith, Mr. Snowden contended that it was useless and absurd to accept the formula 'no annexation' and a the same time to contemplate the retention of 400,000 square miles of territory held by Germany before the war, even on the conditions laid down by Mr. Asquith that this was no militarism, but part of the fulfilment of the divine mission laid on the British people to relieve the oppressed wherever they might be found. (Laughter.) He counselled the democracy to see that the statesmen of this country did not accept the formula 'no annexation' before obtaining from them definite statement as to what they meant by it. It would be delusion and a mockery so long as those statesmen stood by the terms and conditions of the Allied Note to President Wilson. That Note must be repudiated. As understood by the Russian democracy, 'no annexation' did not mean there should be no change of territorial boundaries after the war. If a permanent peace was to be established there would have to be readjustment of territory. The Russian declaration provided that there should be no transfer of territory against the will of the people concerned.

Mr. Roden Buxton said that Russia had caused a great wave of

65

feeling in favour of democratic diplomacy to pass all over the world. Russia was going to work no longer under the old-fashioned methods of secret diplomacy, and had entered into open and free communication with the peoples of the world. In this matter Governments must be the servants, not the masters, of the people. The English people must see to it that in future they were not left in the dark by secret treaties, made in their name but behind their backs.

The resolution was carried with only two dissentients.

The third resolution called upon the Government to proclaim its determination to carry into immediate effect a charter of liberty establishing complete political rights for all men and women, freedom of speech and of the press, and a general amnesty for all political and religious prisoners. This was moved by Mr. C.G. Ammon (British Socialist Party), seconded by Mrs. Despard, supported by Mr. Pethick Lawrence and Mr. Bertrand Russell, and adopted.

Workmen and Soldiers

Mr. W.C. Anderson, M.P., moved the last resolution, calling upon the constituent bodies of the convention to establish local councils of workmen's and soldiers' delegates on the lines of those in Russia, and proposing that the conveners of the convention should be appointed as a provisional committee to assist in the work of organisation. This, he said, he regarded as the 'ugly duckling' of the resolutions. The *Morning Post* had spoken of it as a violation of the law, as an incitement to the subversion of army discipline and military authority. The resolution had no such intention. What they had to say was that soldiers and workmen alike were men, that in the reconstruction of Britain they were alike bound to play a most important part, and that in order to do this they must join hands. It was said that any step on such lines to give expression to the views of soldiers and workmen was in the nature of a revolution. The present Prime Minister had told labour to be audacious – after the war. (Laughter.) If they waited till after the war there would be very little to be audacious about. The peace that would some soon must be a peace made by the people, for the people, and with the stamp of the people upon it. Besides linking together the common interests of soldiers and workmen, such an organisation would strengthen trade unionism and organised labour.

Mr. Robert Williams (Transport Workers), in seconding the resolution, defined its meaning as 'the dictatorship of the proletariat.'

In supporting the resolution, Mrs. Philip Snowden said that one of the most poisonous lies of a perjured press during this war had been the impression it had endeavoured to convey that the movement which those present at the Convention represented was alien, and antagonistic to the soldiers and their interests.

Almost the only definite note of opposition was sounded by Mr. J.L. Toole (Manchester Branch of the National Union of Clerks), who pointed out that there was sufficient organisation already in existence to deal with the various objects specified in the resolution, and that, as this country was suffering from an entirely different set of circumstances from those in Russia, the formation of a committee to co-ordinate the work of the existing labour organisation would be preferable.

The Convention, however, adopted the resolution almost unanimously, and decided to send the following cablegram to the Workmen and Soldiers' Council in Russia:

'The largest and greatest convention of labour, Socialist, and democratic bodies held in Great Britain during this generation has today endorsed Russia's declaration of foreign policy and war aims, and has pledged itself to work through a newly constituted Workmen's and Soldiers' Council for an immediate democratic peace. The Convention received your telegram of congratulation with gratitude and enthusiasm.'

The conveners of the Convention to constitute the nucleus of the Provisional Committee of the new Council are Messrs. H. Alexander, C.G. Ammon, W.C. Anderson, M.P., Mrs. Despard, Messrs. E.C. Fairchild, J. Fineberg, F.W. Jowett, M.P., G. Lansbury, Ramsay MacDonald, M.P., T. Quelch, R. Smillie, Philip Snowden, M.P., and R. Williams.

A request was made from the body of the Convention that thirteen others should also be selected at once by the Convention, but the meeting adopted a recommendation that the Provisional Committee should call district conferences as soon as possible to appoint other members.

Open-Air Meeting Prohibited

In the evening an open-air demonstration was to have been held in Victoria Square, at which Mr. Robert Smillie was to have been the chief speaker. So much feeling had been aroused in the city against the objects of the Convention, particularly the proposition to set up a Council of Workmen's and Soldiers' delegates on the lines of that in Russia, that on Saturday the Home Secretary sent a telegram specially authorising the Lord Mayor and the Chief Constable to prohibit any open-air meeting in connection with the Convention, if they were satisfied it would cause grave disorder. Posters were at once distributed by the Lord Mayor and the Chief Constable prohibiting the holding of the meeting, and the evening demonstration therefore was also held in the Coliseum, though a small section of the delegates in the afternoon clamoured for the outdoor meeting to be held, in order, as was said, to demonstrate that the Convention was determined 'to act as well as talk.'

Police Check Hostile Crowd

The evening demonstration, like the Convention meetings, was only open to ticket-holders. In the course of it an attempt was made by a crowd of some thousands outside to burst the doors open, but a strong force of police, intervened and cleared all the pavements around the building. Large numbers of people however, lined up in Cookridge Street, the main thoroughfare in which the Coliseum stands, and as the audience, about 3,000 strong, emerged there was much booing. The presence of the police, however, prevented any trouble.

An Impression
(By Our Special Representative)
The Herald, 9 June 1917

'This is not a demonstration; it is a conference' said Philip Snowden. He was wrong. It was a demonstration *and* a conference.

As Robert Smillie, the chairman, said, it was the sequel of the recent demonstration in the Albert Hall, London, and his graceful tribute to the promoters of that historic meeting met with the warm approval of the delegates.

The temper of the Leeds demonstration was unmistakeable. Like that of London, it felt a deep impressive thankfulness to Russia, a tremendous joy at a fellow-peoples' emancipation, an almost pathetic yet thrilling hope of a coming world freedom. For Russia has lifted the lid from the hell-pot.

This thing we call the temper of people manifested itself every time Great Britain was mentioned. 'And Ireland! And Ireland!' shouted members of the convention. The oppression of Ireland was evidently resented more than any other present-day injustice.

Superficially, the temper of the demonstration tended towards intolerance when Tupper, of the Seamen's Union, attempted what was a deliberately provocative speech. He demanded that we should obtain indemnities from Germany in order to recompense the widows of British sailors. Incidentally, Williams and Fairchild gave the most effective replies to this plea. 'Get your recompense from your own shipping profiteers', said Williams. 'An indemnity placed on the German working people is another millstone round the necks of the working class' was the substance of Fairchild's retort. But it must be admitted that the delegates would have been wiser to hear Tupper in silence. The natural protests only gave a handle to the unsympathetic Press and to Tupper himself. The truth is that the delegates were well aware of Tupper's intentions. There was no desire to smother opposition, a fact that was demonstrated in the attentive hearing given to the cleverly critical speech of Bevin, of the Dockers' Union, whose opposition was infinitely more pointed and purposeful than Tupper's.

In Perspective

Looking at the proceedings in perspective, such incidents as the storm of applause which greeted the rising of Bertrand Russell and the insistence on his mounting the platform, the receipt of letters from such widely separated public men as Dr. Clifford and James Winstone, of the South Wales Miners, and the rising of the whole Convention in memory of James Connolly, come back to one with peculiar force.

The absence of George Lansbury was sadly felt, and one cannot but regret that the hope expressed in his letter that the Convention should send delegates to meet the Russians was not acted upon, especially in view of the direct invitation which the Convention received by telegram from the Russians. However, it is not too late for the Provisional Committee which was subsequently appointed to respond to the invitation. The reading of the Russian message was the occasion of another outburst of enthusiasm similar to the reception of messages from Lansbury and Clifford Allen, the one from the latter written on the eve of his return to prison.

Smillie's Hand

There were, of course, great moments during the speeches, with which I will deal later, but the Convention did not lack a sense of humour. Smillie created much amusement by holding up his hand each time he requested any dis-sentients to a resolution to signify. There were never more than two or three in opposition, but the humour of the chairman's unconscious action reached its climax when a delegate shouted, 'Put thee hand-down, Bob!' Smillie's hold on the Convention was in a way remarkable. He was looking tired, and the building was not a good one for his rather gentle voice, and it was only his personal hold on the delegates that kept so great a Convention in bounds. His personal popularity was illustrated time and again. 'The Government have taken your leaders,' one speaker deplored. 'Not Bob Smillie,' came the retort from the body of the hall.

Resentment at the prohibition of the open-air public meeting manifested itself several times, and particularly when Scrimgeour from Dundee, urged that the delegates should march from Victoria Square, where the meeting should have been held, to the theatre. The local Labour people, however, had given their word not to attempt an out-of-doors demonstration, and the gathering very reluctantly acquiesced.

Writing of Scrimgeour reminds me of how finely those Scotsmen pronounce the word International – the Inter-r-r-national.

Why, Indeed!

The speeches of the Convention were of a high level. I am aware that all speeches are said to be on a high level. These *were*. Smillie's declaration that the delegates had not met to talk treason but to talk reason was as apt a retort to Press misrepresentation as could have been phrased by anyone. True, Williams later reminded the meeting that in these days reason is treason, but that merely emphasised the point. The growing adherence to the view that there can be no military victory, no knock-out blow, was Smillie's prelude to his case for peace by negotiation. 'When peace comes it will be peace by negotiation', he concluded. 'Then why murder a few more millions of our sons?'

Rarely have I heard Ramsay MacDonald to better effect. 'We offer our congratulations to Russia without drawbacks' was an initial sentence which was followed by thunderous confirmation from the delegates. Unreservedly, without drawbacks, without qualifications, and without 'ifs' the Convention hailed the Russian Revolution. With equal emphasis it expressed its agreement with the total and final destruction of secret diplomacy.

Philip Snowden was as lucid, incisive, and logical as ever, and pleaded strongly for an Allied declaration of war aims. He shattered the feigned misunderstanding of the term annexation. 'It provides for giving to all people the right to dispose of their destinies: Alsace, Poland (and Ireland), and Egypt.'

'The indemnity placed by Germany on France helped the Germans in their imperialism. Any indemnity will help imperialism.' Such was one of the many strong points made by E.C. Fairchild in a speech full of meat. As I have already indicated, the only able speech in opposition was that made by Bevin, and it is doubtful whether Bevin would agree that it was opposition in the full sense of the word. 'If the Allies respond to the Russian call, and Germany fails to respond, then I have no right to be a pacifist, I have a right to fight for the Russian declaration.' Such is one characteristic argument. Bevin also complained that no practical lead was being given [by] the Convention.

C.G. Ammon's plea for efforts to release John Maclean met with much applause, and Tom Mann, speaking from the body of the hall, was loudly cheered for his adherence to Internationalism.

But it was not until the Convention reached the resolution dealing with the establishment of Workers' and Soldiers' Councils in Britain (and Ireland) that it felt it was getting to business. It ceased at this stage to be a demonstration. W.C. Anderson was the mover of the resolution and he was firm on his insistence for a peace made by the people. He emphasised the enormous value that Workers' and Soldiers' Councils could render the discharged and returning soldiers, and replying to the criticism that such bodies would be unconstitutional, declared that they could only be so if the Government made them so.

The Convention was given the lead for which it was anxiously

71

awaiting by Robert Williams, who seconded.

'This means the dictatorship of the proletariat. If any of you have got cold feet go at once. We want the workers to take control of the country. It is theirs by the right of the sacrifices they have made. We speak in the name of our own class and damn the Constitution. We have as little concern for the Constitution as the Russians had for the dynasty of the Romanoffs. If you are sincere about your protestations to Russia go thou and do likewise.' Such are typical sentences.

The resolution was carried with two dissentients, and as a result of an appeal to allow the Conference to add thirteen members to the thirteen convenors who are to form the Provisional Committee of the Workers' and Soldiers' Council it was decided to call district conferences and add thirteen members in that way.

Unquestionably the Conference was a great success. It will give a moral impetus to the movement for a peoples' peace. It has spoken in the name of a big section of Labour for a peace without conquest. It has hailed the Russian Revolution with frankness and it has achieved its object – the establishment of a Follow Russia Movement.

W. H. H[arford].

Some Responses from Trade Unions and their Leaders

Editorial from the National Union of Railwaymen's newspaper *The Railway Review*, 8 June 1917.

During the Whitsuntide week two conferences were held at which two dissimilar bodies discussed and decided with practical unanimity upon attempting to achieve Parliamentary representation. The first was the Co-operative Congress and the other the Commercial Travellers' Association. The co-operators have coquetted with the idea for years, and it was not until they were directly attacked and their interests threatened that they could be brought to make the fateful decision. Neither body has yet officially decided to affiliate to the Labour Party, but we believe this to be only a matter of time. At both conferences the services of the Party were recognised, and strong support to affiliation was foreshadowed. Since then we have seen a movement - or rather a series of movements - which indicate an attempt to supersede Parliamentary methods, and the conference at Leeds on Sunday gave its blessing to the setting up of an outside committee which, if the promoters of the conference mean anything at all, means that this outside organisation will try to control Government from the outside on the model of the Workmen's and Soldiers' Committee in Russia.

In spite of the large attendance and apparent unanimity with which the resolutions were adopted, we do not think such a policy is likely to be successful in this country. Even in Russia the policy has not yet been so successful as to give promise of ultimate triumph, and the difficulties in the way are much greater here. What the conference does indicate, however, is that a split in the Labour forces of the country seems imminent. It is impossible to run two organisations simultaneously with different underlying methods and ideas. Either we shall have to make up our minds to work through Parliament in the ordinary constitutional way, or to leave it alone and seek our objective in some other fashion.

It is significant that the pioneers of the new movement are just those men who have hitherto been strongest in their advocacy of a united Labour Party, and who, because they cannot get their own way there, and are in a hopeless minority, are now seeking to create a new and entirely unauthorised and unconstitutional way of securing it. We are all for democracy against autocracy. But the foundation principle of democracy is majority rule. It is no doubt true that there is some little want of touch between the parts at present, and that the methods of ascertaining the views of the majority are not so perfect as they might be, but the remedy surely lies in making the machinery more elastic and more responsive, and not in creating new organisations which are to supersede the old. If that is done chaos and anarchy alone will be the result. It is not to be denied that a determined minority can make a great deal of trouble and cause a great amount of mischief, but they do not and cannot accomplish much positive good. For that reason we are content to set off the actual work done by and really performed by the organised Trade Unions and their political representatives against the vague ideals preached by those who are responsible for the latest developments. We look forward to an organised working-class movement, working through the unions and through Parliament, as the best and most successful method of securing those reforms both in our social and industrial systems which are necessary. We believe they can secured in that way, and that the signs of success were never so pronounced as they are today. We believe any other method will prove a 'will o' the wisp,' and for that reason we ask the members of the N.U.R. to consider the problem in the light of the historic developments which have proved so successful in the past.

We are not afraid either of new ideas or of new methods, but we want to know whither those ideas and those methods lead. Eventually all these ideas and methods will have to be submitted to the electorate, and that electorate will be a new and enlarged one. It will include the soldiers and the sailors, as well as the industrials, and we are in favour of the electorate deciding upon the Government of the country, and not self-appointed committees who can speak definitely for no body of opinion, and cannot control even the committees they may select.

Report on Leeds Conference by Ben Tillett
Dockers' Record, June 1917

Dear Sirs and Brothers,
The Triennial Meeting sent me along with Bro. Bevin to the so-called Convention held in Leeds. The names of men like Lansbury did give

some reason for at least attending. The Conference, however, was unrepresentative in character; the two organisations responsible for the calling of the meeting were, numerically combined, less than half of our own members. Even in this case the members of each of the organisations had not been consulted. The resolutions were jockeyed by a few without any serious attempt being made to face the realities of the war and its obligations. On the top of this piece of 'sharp practice' no amendments were allowed to be discussed in a so-called democratic conference! So far as the delegates were concerned none of them had any authority to agree with the resolutions laid down, and most of them had no authority to represent other than their own opinions, which, however, in the case of this Conference were not allowed ventilation. There were between four and five hundred delegates present (some of them of alien origin) who were under twenty-six years of age. As far as the character of the Conference is concerned, outside of platitudes, there was not the slightest attempt made to face the issues of war, or suggest terms, conditions or solutions. The viciousness of the whole business was manifest in cant and cynicism. The embodiment of these features of the Conference was personified in the person of the mover of the first resolution. The person most responsible for the retarding of progress and initiative, J.R. MacDonald, delivered a revolutionary speech; such a speech, conning from the late statesman of the Labour Party, lent a Pecksniffian sententiousness to the discussion, coming as the sentiment did from a man and his colleagues who have calmly stood by without sympathy or interest in the fact that thousands and scores of thousands of our soldiers' bodies were being torn to tatters by shrapnel and high explosives, that Russian soldiers were being murdered by the hundred thousand because of the absence of ammunition, some of the regiments not having ammunition, or even rifles, or in some cases only one rifle between three men, others one rifle between five men. Never a word uttered, but sinister and underground checks put upon supply. Our sailors have been murdered on the high seas by the thousand, yet never a word of help. In the dark days of insufficient supplies, when Russia, France and ourselves were in panic at the wholesale destruction of our soldiers' lives, these men cynically sat silent. Wrapped in their own impenetrable cant, they imagine the Russian workmen do not know of their guilt, the real blood-guilt of pro-Germanism. The blunders of our Government and, the malignity of these new revolutionaries (?) have resulted in the loss of a million Russian lives and half a million of our own soldiers, not a single man of whom was the cause or party to the war. It has never dawned on the atrophied pro-Germanism of their minds that war is paid for in blood and labour by the workers, ninety-six per cent of whom make up the fighting forces. Some of us who have loved and worked with Prince Kropotkin are amazed at the impertinence of the new-found zeal of these men. The Buxton incident was well contrived. The reference to our late comrade Connolly struck a tragic note, and the audience for the first and only time felt the meaning of the Irish Movement. But Connolly's memory was dishonoured in association with the people who called the Conference. At least, and however wrong-headed it might have been, Connolly died as he had lived for his country, but these people appear to have no country. In conclusion I want to say:

(1) That first and last Russia's real interests and the aims of the Russian Revolutionaries were never stated.

(2) The Conference did not represent working-class opinion and was rigged by a middle-class element, more mischievous than important.

(3) No offer of help, or method, or suggestion was forthcoming to assist to end the war, so far as the Russian Movement is concerned.

(4) No reference was made to the pillage and murder and disaster inflicted on the Russians by the Germans.

(5) The movers of the meeting expressed neither regret nor shame at their previous sinister altitude while munitions were short, while capitalistic sordidness stood as a menace to Government endeavour and military and naval necessities. While all our Union members have zealously worked and helped in the interests of the workers forming twenty-four out of twenty-five of the fighting forces, without love or desire for war, but simply that our own class should be saved the worst effects of war, these people have played the assassins, alike to us, to Russia and to the French, whose armies are made up in the same proportions as our own. Some of those who spoke have begrudged the meagre allowance to the soldiers' dependents, and have fought against women's wages being fair. So

far from the Conference helping a solution in the midst of this bloody Armageddon, it has been merely a stage army of fiddling Neros unconscious of its cant.

Yours sincerely,
Ben Tillett,
General Secretary, Dock, Wharf, Riverside and General Workers' Union of Great Britain and Ireland

Short Report on the Leeds Convention by delegates from the Postal and Telegraph Clerk's Association
Executive Circular, 30 July 1917.

Dear Colleagues,

Leeds Convention

Acting upon your instructions we attended the Conference at Leeds on the 3rd June, called to hail the Russian Revolution and to organise the British Democracy to follow Russia. It was announced that up to noon 1150 delegates were in attendance and that others were coming. The delegates represented Trades Councils and Local Labour Parties, 209; Trade organisations, 371, I.L.P. 294; B.S.P. 88; other Socialists societies, 16; womens organisations 54; other organisations 118. Mr. R. Smillie occupied the chair. Four resolutions were submitted dealing with (1) The Hailing of the Russian Revolution (2) Foreign Policy and War Aims to be in agreement with those of Russia. (3) Civil liberties. (4) The formation of Workmens and Soldiers Councils on the lines of Russia in order generally to give effect to the policy determined by the Conference.

By decision of the Conference no amendments were admitted. Your delegates voted in favour of the first three resolutions but found themselves unable to vote on the final resolution in the absence of any indication that existing trade organisations would be co-ordinated for the purposes of the resolution. The whole of the resolutions were carried unanimously except the last one to which there were a few dissentients.

J.F. Hunter, W.J. Baker

Advertisements in The Herald *for the new booklet*
What Happened at Leeds, *June 1917*

The Aftermath

Janet Douglas and Christian Høgsbjerg

After Leeds, different forces tried to take the movement forward, but what this movement meant was not as clear as it might seem, and the general spirit of unity at the Convention was not destined to last long. The conservative approach of some trade union leaders soon manifested itself and, as early as 5 June at a specially convened conference in London, the National Sailors' and Firemen's Union (represented at the Leeds Convention by Edward Tupper) voted to prevent British representatives from sailing to a planned peace conference in Stockholm.[22] Tupper apparently felt greatly insulted by the lack of respect shown to him at the Convention. He personally travelled to Aberdeen to persuade seafarers to stop a delegation of Labour, ILP and BSP members (including Ramsay MacDonald, Fred Jowett and Edwin Fairchild) sailing to Petrograd on the invitation of the Petrograd Soviet and provisional Russian government to discuss the prospects of a 'people's peace'.[23] As the Fabian Beatrice Webb commented in her diary on 7 June,

> The thousand or more delegates to the Leeds conference were, so one of them declared, 'mentally drunk', and quite incapable of coherent thinking. They were swayed by emotions: an emotion towards peace and an emotion towards workers' control. It is an odd irony that the concrete example of 'workers' control' arising out of the Leeds conference was the seamen's refusal to permit MacDonald and [G.H.] Roberts [M.P.] to proceed to Petrograd to forward the propaganda for a negotiated peace![24]

As Sylvia Pankhurst and Philip Snowden agreed, the Convention had been a 'mass of conglomerate elements, not yet fused, lacking as yet a common policy or plan of action'.[25] The only real resolution pointing to concrete action was the fourth, calling for the formation of Workmen's and Soldiers' Councils, which had been carried overwhelmingly amidst much excitement. But the one specific aim of the new Councils was to look after disabled soldiers, hardly posing an existential threat to the capitalist state. More critically, Noah Ablett, representing South Wales miners at the Convention, noted the absence of 'some sort of programme, some sort of practical suggestion of how

79

we are to set up the Councils'.[26] This was not so surprising, perhaps, because as J.T. Murphy later wrote, 'no one present had any knowledge whatever of the history of the Russian working-class movement, its party struggles or its leaders' and knew 'next to nothing about how Workers' and Soldiers' Councils were constituted and had only the vaguest ideas as to the conditions in which they could and should be formed'.[27] As Stephen White notes, W.C. Anderson, who apparently initiated the resolution to set up Workmen's and Soldiers' Councils actually 'indicated that he and his colleagues now felt that it would be best to obtain the government's consent to the formation of the Councils before proceeding further'. Anderson himself stressed the resolution was 'not intended to be subversive of military responsibilities' and, as Murphy reflected later, there was 'no evidence of the existence at that time of any attempt to permeate the armed forces with revolutionary ideas'.[28]

Bertrand Russell articulated his worries about all this in a private letter on 5 June:

> I got back from Leeds yesterday. It was a wonderful occasion, but a little disappointing from the point of view of practical outcomes. Snowden and MacDonald and Anderson are not the right men – they have not the sense for swift dramatic action. The right man would be Williams (of the Transport Workers), but he is not yet sufficiently prominent. Smillie is perfect except he is too old. The enthusiasm and all-but unanimity were wonderful – out of 2,500, there were only about three dissentients. Nothing was lacking except leaders…[29]

Indeed, despite the fact that the appointed provisional committee elected from the Convention had among its duties to 'assist the formation of the local Workmen's and Soldiers' Councils', this was later quietly shelved by the national Council leadership in favour of focusing on a more electoral strategy of trying, as Lansbury's paper *The Herald* put it, to develop a 'New Charter for the workers' and put a 'People's Party' into office. This was, Lansbury noted, the 'great patriotic duty' coming out of the Leeds Convention, and he expressed concern lest workers' discontent, which was 'seething all over the place', should break out instead in 'undirected and sporadic forms'.[30] The Leeds Convention took place just after a mass wave of unofficial strike action by over 200,000 workers across the munitions industry in May, a strike which represented a total of 1.5 million days and encompassed 48 towns and cities. Just after the May strikes ended, Lord Derby, the Minister of War, wrote to General Haig, British Commander-in-Chief in France, noting that 'the Russian Revolution has created an unrest which is revolutionary and dangerous'.[31] As Ramsay MacDonald noted in an article written after the Convention, the aim of such a display of radicalism at the Leeds Convention was about ensuring that the rising working-class discontent could subsequently be channelled into safe directions: 'Before the war I felt that what was called "the spirit of the rebel" was to a great extent a stagey pose. It is now required to save us.'[32] MacDonald later regretted his participation in Leeds, but as one contemporary noted, at the time 'anyone on the Left who did not swim with the new current was likely to be swept aside'.[33]

Snowden in his autobiography recalled that the proposal 'for the establishment of Workmen's and Soldiers' Councils was the idea of Mr. W.C. Anderson'.

> For some days before the Convention the Press had seized upon this resolution and had grossly misrepresented its purpose. It was described as an incitement to the subversion of army discipline and military authority. It was in effect a very harmless resolution as a careful reading of its terms will show. It was largely unnecessary, for the work of looking after the interests of the workers in industry and of the disabled soldiers was undertaken by an organisation conducted by the Labour Party and the Trade Unions. Nothing came of this resolution, as, when the committee which had organised the Conference met afterwards, we considered it was unnecessary to carry out the proposal.[34]

Though Snowden slightly simplifies matters here, the Provisional Committee did subsequently make it clear that the Councils were to serve 'primarily as a propagandist body, not as a rival to, or to supplant any of the existing working-class organizations, but to infuse into them a more active sense of liberty' – in other words, a far cry from the implicit challenge to the state represented by the Soviets in Russia.[35] Though district conferences of the Workmen's and Soldiers' Councils did take place in most of the thirteen designated areas, and elected a Provisional Committee which met alongside a full National Council (which finally met to hold one meeting in October 1917), by June 1917 the British government was preparing how best to counter any such movement. As Lord Milner wrote to Lloyd George on 1 June, it was too late to stop the Leeds Convention, but the Press could be instructed 'not to "boom" the Leeds proceedings too much', and 'some strong steps to stop the "rot" in this country' would have to be considered 'unless we wish to "follow Russia" into impotence and dissolution'.[36] A 'National War Aims Committee' directed by the spy and novelist, John Buchan, was established in July 1917 and, as Lloyd George put it bluntly in August, 'The Nation has chosen its own Workmen's and Soldiers' Committee and that is the House of Commons. We cannot allow sectional organisations to direct the war or dictate the peace'.[37]

Despite government bans on some attempts to convene local and district Council meetings, a brave attempt was made from below to build the Council movement, despite the Labour Party Executive resolving, in July 1917, that it had 'nothing to do with the Leeds Convention' and 'no local organisation affiliated to the Labour Party ought to convene Conferences which are not in harmony with the general policy of the Party as laid down in its Annual Conferences'.[38] As Snowden recalled, 'a number of local conferences had already been called to take up the question of forming local branches of Workmen's and Soldiers' Councils', but they often encountered venue cancellations, local opposition and 'organised rowdyism' on the part of mobs encouraged by newspapers such as the *Daily Mail* and *Daily Express* and often organised by the British Workers League, founded in 1916 as a 'patriotic labour' group and partly funded by Lord Milner. Perhaps most notably on 28 July 1917, a Workers' and Soldiers' Council meeting at the Brotherhood Church in Southgate, North London was broken up by a 200-300 strong violent crowd led by overseas soldiers singing 'Rule Britannia'.[39] One of those present was Bertrand Russell, who recalled the experience in a letter later that day, as being 'really very horrible … the young soldiers were pathetic, thinking we were their enemies. They all believed we were in the pay of the Kaiser.'

> At one moment they all made a rush at me, and I was in considerable danger
> – but a woman (I don't know who) hurled herself between me and them.
> They hesitated to attack her – and then the police appeared. She showed
> wonderful courage.

In his *Autobiography*, Russell told the following amusing story about this incident:

> Two of the drunken viragos began to attack me with their boards full of nails. While I was wondering how one defended oneself against this type of attack, one of the ladies went up to the police and suggested that they should defend me. The police, however, merely shrugged their shoulders. 'But he is an eminent philosopher', said the lady, and the police still shrugged. 'But he is famous all over the world as a man of learning', she continued. 'But he is the brother of an earl', she finally cried. At this, the police rushed to my assistance.[40]

On 29 July in Swansea, about 200 delegates mainly from South Wales assembled for a district conference to discuss the Council movement, but again this meeting was violently broken up by a 500 strong pro-war crowd before it began and the delegates dispersed.[41] In Leeds, it was announced that a Yorkshire conference would meet on 25 August and after 'lively' discussion, Leeds Trades Council agreed to send three delegates. Amazingly the venue was to be the Albert Hall. Again this was withdrawn and on the 3 August, the *Yorkshire Post*, under the headline 'Pacifist Conference in Difficulties in Leeds', reported that the conference organisers were experiencing difficulties in finding a suitable hall. The situation rapidly descended into what, depending on your point of view, was farce or intrigue. The organisers approached the Watch Committee to hold the conference in the crypt of the Town Hall, a booking the Watch Committee accepted on 21 August, as long as the meeting was not prohibited. Next day it was announced that the meeting was banned on instructions from the Home Office.[42]

As White notes, in August 1917, Arthur Henderson's resignation from Lloyd George's Government, on the grounds that he was now supporting putative peace efforts, 'allowed the Labour Party to recapture a measure of political independence and to contain this movement', directing the hopes of peace towards trying to re-convene the Socialist International, which had collapsed in ignominy in 1914. The momentum soon went out of the campaign for Councils, and a government intelligence report noted that by mid-October 1917 'the Workmen's and Soldiers' Council movement was moribund'. In Leeds, for example, the local Trades Council considered a 'lengthy communication' from the district representative of the Workers' and Soldiers' Council on 24 October 1917, but unanimously resolved that the propaganda work of the Council 'can and will be done best by the existing Labour organizations'.[43]

The Call to the Council

The Herald, 23 June 1917

WE put forward this week a programme which we submit as the logical interpretation of the resolutions adopted at the Leeds Conference. We claim for this interpretation, of course, no dogmatic finality. It is a basic article of our creed that difference of opinion about practical details is no bar to union over essentials. The very last thing which we desire is in any way to 'split off' any section from any of the existing organisations which are working for democratic ends. But this general largeness of idea is by no means to be identified with a vague and sentimental sloppiness of thought. Unity of aim is not the same as indefiniteness of programme: it is almost the opposite. There is one gulf - one real gulf which no idealism can bridge - and that is the gulf between the people who really passionately desire *the next step* and those who are content to wait upon events. It used to be commonly said that there were two types of social reformer - those who agitated for some minor but immediate amelioration and those who dreamed of an ultimate but apparently unattainable Utopia. Both types were useful, were necessary. But the lesson of the Russian Revolution is that the two types can easily become one, and that when they become one they become invincible. The Leeds Conference claimed to be following up the example of Russia. It voiced demands. The test of its purpose and reality is whether it follows up those demands by insisting upon their realisation. Russia has shown us the way. Russia has shown us that nothing is impossible. Our own bureaucrats and capitalists have hailed the triumph of Russian idealism. With what face, then, can they even attempt to deprecate ours? When we framed Utopias before, we were told that the machinery to work our schemes would always be lacking. But Russia has found machinery. It is true that that machinery is still imperfect; but it is better than what it replaced - better even from the most immediately practical point of view. Before the Revolution the Russian workers were starving because of the machinations of the profiteers: the food was there, and they knew it was there, but they could not get it. They have got it now. *We* have all along, ever since the birth of industrialism, been told that wealth sufficient to ensure the decencies of life to the masses was not available. The war has proved that that was a mere falsehood. We know now that a bare half of the effective labour power of the nation can produce enough to keep the nation going and at the same time to provide most of the incredible expenditure of war. Nothing could be a surer proof of the claim we always advanced that the workers were being cheated of their birth-right. The wealth is *there*; it is only a question of taking it. We used to be told that we had no machinery for regulating production and distribution - that 'the expropriation of the capitalist' was a mere phrase, since, when the Capitalist was gone, there would be no means left of organising industry. We have got the machinery now. It is coming into being daily by the natural development of industry. Does anybody pretend that the control exercised by the State during war over railways, munitions, shipping, and coal, could not be transformed, with a minimum of re-organisation, into State ownership? Does anybody pretend that, if that were done, the menace of bureaucracy could not be effectively met by the *management* of mines by the Miners' Federation, the *management* of railways by the N.U.R., and so forth? There is no difficulty about doing these things; it remains only to do them. The Council set up by the Leeds Conference is *there* - or, to be strictly accurate, it will be there when the thirteen additional representatives have been elected, which is only a matter of a few weeks now - to see that the demands of the workers are met. It has behind it a force - industrial, material, moral - which makes its demands irresistible. We were reminded at Leeds that the gathering was a *Conference*, not a *Demonstration*. It was there to inaugurate action, not to talk; and if it fails to inaugurate action it will have failed altogether. But it will not fail. Next month the elections come. Those who stand for election must stand on a programme; all of us must be hammering out the programme for which we hope the votes will be cast. The programme put forward in this paper claims to be the sort of thing that all the people want. That is why we call it 'plans for the people's party.' We are not referring in that phrase to any novel or sectional organisation, but to the great common enthusiasm in which the various parties already working for the greater power and prosperity of the people meet. Every individual, of course, has his own views on this or that: difference of opinion, discussion, propaganda, are the very life-blood of progress. We do not suggest for one moment that everyone

86

who voted for the Leeds resolutions would endorse every particular of our suggestions: but the Leeds resolutions meant something like this or they meant nothing at all.

Take for a moment some of the items in our programme which no malignancy or mendacity can pretend to be not immediately practicable. 'Great increase of old-age pensions.' Why not? Everybody knows it is right: everybody knows it is possible. It is left undone simply because our present Government have not the common humanity to do it. 'Increase of soldiers' pay.' Why not? Australia and New Zealand already pay their soldiers, roughly, five times what we pay ours! 'Freedom of speech and Press.' This is an elementary right passionately desired by the people. *It fails to be secured solely for lack of a body whose special business is to insist upon securing it.* What greater justification for the creation of the new Council could we need? The same with the release of political prisoners - some of whom are going through experiences nothing short of actual torture for doing what they think right. Nobody except a few Prussian-minded oligarchs wants them to be tortured. The British mind is on the whole a fair and generous one, and respects courage and conviction even when it differs from the particular opinions held by those who are suffering for their convictions. Certainly *Labour*, even such of it as is out of sympathy with the conscientious objector, does not want to see militarism empowered to grind freedom of conscience under its heel: *for Labour knows that militarism is always planning to grind Labour under its heel.* The Prussianism which is now rampant in the land is most bitterly resented. Those who think everything subservient to the war, and therefore feel inhibited from a direct protest, resent it, if anything, more bitterly than the pacifists, who at any rate have the relief of coming out in direct opposition; those who support the war on the ground that it is a war for freedom feel tricked and betrayed, outraged and violated, every time their support is used to trample upon freedom at home. Parliament, stale and un-representative, has abrogated its functions. Government rests entirely in the hands of a few men who have always been bitterly opposed to liberty and democracy in all their forms. The military autocracy has a free hand, and it has not the sense to use its power with even a pretence of fairness or moderation: it it is too often truculent, insulting, contemptuous, 'Prussian.'

One great patriotic duty lies before the Council. Discontent is seething all over the place. It is the first maxim of statesmanship that popular discontent never exists without a cause: it is the first task of statesmanship to remove the cause. The narrow sectionalism of our rulers seems incapable of statesmanship - hence the danger that the unrest may break out in undirected and sporadic forms. The Council will be able to save the nation from that waste and disaster. It will be able to remove unrest by insisting upon the causes of unrest being removed. But it must insist. It must act. Our part is to support its action.

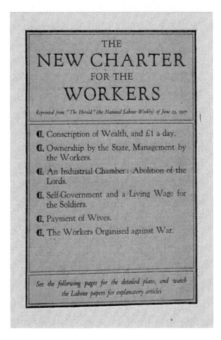

THE
NEW CHARTER
FOR THE
WORKERS

Reprinted from "The Herald" (the National Labour Weekly) of June 23, 1917

℄ Conscription of Wealth, and £1 a day.

℄ Ownership by the State, Management by the Workers.

℄ An Industrial Chamber: Abolition of the Lords.

℄ Self-Government and a Living Wage for the Soldiers.

℄ Payment of Wives.

℄ The Workers Organised against War.

See the following pages for the detailed plans, and watch the Labour papers for explanatory articles

Plans for the People's Party [Later published as a *Herald* pamphlet, *The New Charter for the Workers*]
The Herald, 23 June 1917

Foreword
WHAT ARE WE going to DO? We have had the Albert Hall. We have had Leeds. We have set up the Soldiers' and Workers' Council. We have shown emotion, enthusiasm, determination. What are we going to do? Thirteen districts will next month elect representatives to the Central

Council. What will they do? What will they help the Council to do? It is the business of every one of us to be thinking about a practical programme. We cannot be satisfied with formulas; we must translate the principles, aspirations, battle-cries of the Leeds Convention into a plan of immediate action. The following programme we believe to be thorough, bold, practical. It is put forward as a contribution to the deliberations of the Council and to the framing of an election policy for the district representatives.

Economic

Conscription of Wealth and Equality of Income

(a) Expropriation of private landowners and capitalists. No compensation beyond an ample provision against individual hardship.

(b) All men and women willing to work to be paid, even when their work happens to be not needed, just as soldiers are paid when they are not fighting. Equal payment for all to be the result at which re-organisation shall aim.

(c) Instead of the present capitalistic methods of production **Ownership by the State: Management by the Workers.**

This shall be applied immediately to the case of Mines, Railways, Shipping, Shipbuilding, and Engineering, Electric Light and Power, Gas and Water.

(d) The National properties in Mines, Railways, Shipping, Land so created to be leased to the Unions on conditions which will ensure every member at present money value a **Minimum Real Income of One Pound a Day**.

Economic Independence of all Men and Women.

Until such time as the whole industry of the country can be organised upon the basis indicated above, the workers in industries not embraced in the above list - including those whose work is that of the household and the bringing up of children - shall be assured a similar standard of life by one, or a combination, of the following means:

(a) A high minimum wage guaranteed by the State through a levy upon the profits of unexpropriated capitalists.

89

(b) Continuation and increase of present war allowances to the women and children of soldiers' families,

(c) Increase of maternity benefits and maintenance of children during school age.

(d) Great increase of old-age pensions beginning at an earlier age than at present.

(e) Revision of war and other pensions periodically in accordance with the increased cost of living.

(f) Increase of soldiers' pay to Australian, Canadian and New Zealand standards.

Provision against hardship occasioned by the first expropriation shall be made by means of a levy upon the yet unexpropriated capitalists. Those classes who have sanctioned and approved the conscription of men cannot on any moral ground object to the conscription of money - expropriation of property owners for national purposes. Indeed the latter has justifications which cannot be invoked for the former. Not only must we assure to all our workers an income on which a reasonable life can be led: we must also create conditions in which work ceases to be mere drudgery under a ruling class, whether of bureaucrats or of capitalists. By taking over the management of industry the workers will be realising freedom and democracy in their daily labour. The nationalisation of industry will not subject the workers to the discipline of a bureaucratic machine, but enable them through the Unions to organise production in the interest of all. State ownership of the means of production, balanced by the control of industry by organised Labour, offers the best, and indeed the only guarantee of individual freedom in an industrial society. In the case of the Post Office we already have the first half of the principle - ownership by the State - and there is now a powerful movement towards the second half - management by the workers. As to the practicability of the minimum income indicated above, the economic facts of the war prove conclusively that a minimum real income of a pound a day, present value, for every worker is quite attainable. The country is spending eight millions a day on the war alone. Very nearly the whole of the wealth represented by that sum, together with the wealth necessary for the support of the civilian population, is created by the labour of not much more than eight million workers. In peace time there are not more than fifteen million available workers, including men, women and children. More than half of this number is now withdrawn for the army or unproductive army work, like munitions. Making every allowance for such of the army as do productive work, the support of the army and the country now falls upon half the usual available workers, the half which includes the older people and the children. This calculation is not seriously affected by the argument that we are 'living on credit.' It is not true, in the sense that we are consuming wealth that we are not now creating, save to a very tiny extent. The amount that America sends to us 'on credit' is about offset by the amount that we send to our Allies 'on credit.' And although the Government may pay for its purchases by money borrowed from the capitalist, that is merely in order to preserve the capitalist system. The actual material - munitions, clothing, etc. - is made by the workers now, not taken by some magic from past or future stores. And while it may be true that we are making war material instead of renewing necessary plant, we have official assurance that that is so only to a small extent. The experience of the war shows that, given a large and insistent demand - ensured during the last three years by the immense consumption of war - the wealth necessary to satisfy it can be produced far more easily than was generally supposed. The high consumption ensured during the last three years by war, must after the war be ensured by the high standard of living of the workers. Those now busy destroying good houses in France and Belgium must after the war be kept busy destroying bad ones in the slums and in building better ones; and in all the work of readjustment and reconstruction necessary to ensure food and raw material, and a continually increasing productivity in order to meet the continually increasing consumption of the workers.

Political

A Complete Democracy

(a) Abolition of the House of Lords. Substitution for it of a Chamber based on the representation, not of geographical areas, but of occupations, industrial, professional and domestic, Labour and Professional bodies thus becoming a constituent part of the country's government.

Political and industrial reconstruction cannot be considered in complete abstraction from each other, and it is essential to any plan, even of political reconstruction, that the workers should have their own industrial Chamber - representative not of geographical areas, like the House of Commons, but of occupations, industries and professions. This body must sit, not for a few days in every year, but continuously. It must not merely pass resolutions and indicate policies, but have definite powers of initiative and control. It will represent the people in their capacity of producers, just as the present House of Commons is supposed to represent them, and as a reformed House of Commons will really represent them, in the capacity of consumers.

(b) Abolition of all titles and State-granted honours.

The traffic in titles has become a financial and moral premium upon reactionary politics, as well as a subtle form of State bribery.

(c) Full political rights for all men and women. Payment of Election expenses.

(d) Democratisation of Army and Navy (so long as they exist) by the effective representation of the Rank and File in all military and naval administrations not dealing with strategy. Abolition of military discipline in its present form immediately on the conclusion of peace. [Demobilisation may last two or three years after the declaration of peace. During that time, unless the law is modified, men who had enlisted for the duration of the war may still be subject to restrictive forms of discipline and to the risk of being used for strike-breaking, etc.] The Laws framed for the purpose of providing for Freedom of Conscience to be made effective. Freedom of Speech and Press. The Right to Strike, and to advocate strikes.

Social

The Opportunity to Enjoy Life

(a) A freer Social Life: Increase of opportunities for Recreation, Sports, Clubs. Better Public-Houses.

(b) A high minimum standard of comfort to be set in all housing and similar schemes.

(c) Education, both elementary and secondary, to be universal. No child labour, but maintenance of children during school age; small classes; immediate large increases in salaries of teachers.

We put education under 'enjoyment of life' because it is clear that the proper end of education is the proper enjoyment of life. The present outcry for better scientific and technical training, for the endowment of research in processes which may be adapted to commercial ends, and for similar so-called 'educational' developments, will miss the real educational end if, by centring exclusively upon mechanical or industrial efficiency, it disregards the necessity for leisure and enjoyment. The problem of education is not how to contribute to the production of greater material wealth, but how to nourish in every individual the desire for a full free life (since without that desire there is no hope of social progress) and the capacity for enjoying a full free life (since without that capacity social progress is unmeaning). That part of education in this country which is known as 'higher' has, in spite of its narrowness, at least one good point: it aims at being a liberal education - an education which is an end in itself, and not a mere means to 'efficiency.' This aim must be kept in view by education of all grades and all kinds.

Foreign Policy

The Workers Organised Against War

(a) Communications between workers to be maintained in War as in Peace.

(b) Negotiations to be instituted at once to end the present war on the following basis:

The right of all people to decide their own destiny.

No indemnities, but each belligerent to restore the damage he has done, or to compound such reparation by concessions to be agreed by negotiation.

Equal access by all peoples to the trade and raw materials of the world.

The government of non-European races in Africa to be regarded as an international trust, with no exclusive advantages to the sovereign state; such populations not to be trained for war or subject to conscription or servile labour.

All secret treaties, or treaties not ratified by the people to be void.

Disarmament by International Agreement.

Conclusion

If democracy is to be a reality in the future, the competition for preponderant military power, which necessarily militarises all the nations taking part in it, must be brought to an end. But the attempt on the part of one nation to create over vast areas of the world special reserves for its own trade and industry, or to block therein the access of other nations to necessary raw materials, will be certain, sooner or later, to be resisted by military means. These conflicts, though the workers as a whole never benefit from them, are the main source of modern wars. The price of peace is equality of economic opportunity for all nations big and little. If the arming of the black millions of Africa for the purpose of fighting the white man's quarrels is permitted, a new danger as well as a new horror will be added to civilisation. If a people is not fit to share the privileges of the British Empire in the shape of self-government it should not be asked to share its burdens by fighting its wars. Forced fighting, like forced labour, is in such case, whatever it may be elsewhere, undisguised slavery. The only certain cure for war is disarmament. If the nations are not loaded they will not explode.

Workers. These proposals are possible of immediate realisation. Have audacity. Do not look back to the old conditions. To this generation has come the opportunity of centuries. Seize it. The responsibility upon each one of you is enormous. In Russia the Council of Soldiers' and Workers' Delegates is building a new world for the workers. It is in your power now to do the same here. Unite in your Workers' and Soldiers' Councils and use your power.

Editorial on the Russian Revolution and Leeds Convention from *The Socialist Review*

[an Independent Labour Party journal edited by
James Ramsay MacDonald] 15 July 1917.

The Convention of Delegates from Trade Union, Socialist, and Democratic organisations held at Leeds on Sunday, June 3, has broken the deadly spell that has held the Labour movement dumb and submissive to its official leaders since the outbreak of the war. The fact of such a huge gathering of delegates having assembled and with virtual unanimity adopted resolutions wholly at variance with the spirit and the letter of the official policy, has stirred the ranks of Labour throughout the country with a sense of relief and self-realisation. The Convention was held in acknowledged defiance not only of the disapproval of the Government group of Labour leaders, but of the angry protests of the war press, which openly incited the authorities and the mob to prevent the meeting. It was called by a joint Socialist Committee consisting of Mr. Ramsay MacDonald, Philip Snowden, F.W. Jowett, W.C. Anderson, from the I.L.P., Robert Smillie and George Lansbury, and British Socialist Party delegates, whose names were printed on the circulars sent broadcast to local Trade Union branches and Trades Councils. Its avowed purpose was to hail the Russian Revolution and endorse its charter of civil liberties, its declaration against conquest and annexations, and to appeal to the democracies to work for an agreement between the international democracies for a general peace, and to call into being local Workmen and Soldiers' Councils to agitate on these lines. The fact that a Convention of such a nature should not only have been held, and successfully brought together over 1,100 delegates from all parts of the country, but should have signalised itself by enthusiastically cheering the speakers in proportion to their repute as 'traitors' and the pacifist and revolutionary quality of their speeches is, we repeat, a notable sign of working-class revulsion against the whole militarist and industrial policy of the Government, which the Trade Union Executive, Members of Parliament, and Labour Ministers have so docilely supported. And, what is no less important, it is an unmistakable and warning sign of the spreading feeling of Labour revolt in the country.

The Labour Party and the Future

What the probable developments of the Workmen and Soldiers' Council movement may be, and what effect the new organisation may have on the present Labour Party as the political instrument of Labour, it is impossible to forecast. But it may safely be predicted that unless the Labour Party speedily severs its alliance with the Government, resumes its independence, and sets about vigorously following the lead which it ought itself to have taken, it will discover very soon that the workers have discarded it as a broken reed. There would, indeed, have been no immediate need for the Leeds Convention had not the Trade Union M.P.s and the majority of the Labour Party Executive abrogated their functions and scrapped their Labour Party principles. As it is, the Government gang of Labour leaders no more represent the actual Labour movement in the country to-day than do dubs of stagnant water on the foreshore the great flowing sea. But, in truth, the complete collapse of the Labour Party in the present crisis demonstrates what has long been pretty evident to observers, that a party dominated by Trade Union officials, promoted not for their political opinions or capacity, but for Trade Union services, the majority of whom are destitute of enthusiasm or idealism, can never adequately voice and urge forward the needs and aspirations of the democracy. Even Trade Union workers do not live by Trade Union prescriptions alone.

The Seamen's Executive's Folly

Space only permits us a brief note on the action of the Executive of the Seamen and Firemen's Union in preventing Mr. Ramsay MacDonald, M.P., Mr. Fred Jowett, M.P., and Mr. Fairchild from visiting Petrograd in response to the invitation of the Russian Workmen and Soldiers' Council. The conduct of the Seamen's Executive in having recourse for such a purpose to a mean and tyrannical use of their Trade Union power has but served to completely discredit the policy and pretentions of pro-war Labour politicians in this country. The episode reveals how receptive the reactionary Labour mind is becoming to the spirit and methods of Prussian Junkerdom. Perhaps, too, it affords a not unneeded warning against the supposition that Trade Union bureaucracy would, had it the opportunity, prove a lesser menace than capitalist autocracy to the civil liberties of the nation. Meanwhile, the Russian Workmen and Soldiers Council has sent warm expressions of sympathy to Mr. MacDonald, Mr. Jowett, and Mr. Fairchild, and is more urgent than ever that they should come to Petrograd. Meanwhile, also, the Rt. Hon. Arthur Henderson in Petrograd has frankly informed the British Government that unless the Socialist delegates are allowed to proceed to Petrograd it would be quite impolitic for Mr. G.H. Roberts, M.P., or any other pro-Government Labour delegates to go there.

Workers' and Soldiers' Council
Leeds Convention (circular), 15 June 1917[44]

Workers' & Soldiers' Council

COMRADES,

In accord with the spirit and purpose of the magnificent and inspiring Convention held at Leeds on Sunday, June 3rd, the members of the Provisional Committee then appointed have met, and agreed upon the preliminary arrangements required to give effect to the decisions of the Convention.

The Convention resolved that 13 directly elected representatives should be added to the acting Provisional Committee.

The acting Provisional Committee therefore proposes to divide the area of Great Britain and Ireland into 13 districts. The districts are as follows:—

1.	Scotland, E.	Edinburgh
2.	„ W.	Glasgow
3.	N.E.	Newcastle
4.	Yorkshire	Leeds
5.	Lancashire, Cheshire & N. Wales	Manchester
6.	N. & E. Midlands	Leicester
7.	S. & W. „	Birmingham
8.	East Anglia	Norwich
9.	London & Home Counties	London
10.	Southern Counties	Southampton
11.	E. Wales and Environs of Bristol	Cardiff
12.	Wales, W.	Swansea
13.	Ireland.	

In each district, on a Saturday in July, the Provisional Committee will hold a District Conference in the towns set out above.

At each District Conference there will be elected one representative of the District to serve upon the Provisional Committee of the Workers' and Soldiers' Council. The

98

Council of Workers' and Soldiers' Delegates, 'Manifesto to District Conferences (circular)', 1917[45]

District Conferences will deal with other business to be indicated later, when full particulars as to date, the precise place of meeting, &c., will be announced.

You are especially requested **to note that the District Conferences will be convened by the Provisional Committee** of the Workers' and Soldiers' Council now sitting in London.

It is urgently and imperatively requested that every person by whom this circular is read will send to the Secretary of the Workers' and Soldiers' Council, a list of all Labour, Socialist and Democratic Organisations, political and industrial, including Workshop Committees, Committees of Shop Stewards, and other working class organisations known to be established in any part of the country. Wherever possible, the names and addresses of the secretaries of these local bodies should be given.

The Provisional Committee of the Workers' and Soldiers' Council will then compile a complete list of all the bodies specified above, group them in accordance with the plan of territorial division, and then invite each organisation to appoint delegates to attend the District Conference.

All delegates to the Leeds Convention are urged to work through their organisations to secure co-ordination in promoting **Demonstrations** in support of the decisions of the Convention.

The exceptional facilities open to Trades Councils and local Labour Parties for the promotion of Demonstrations should be utilised to the fullest extent possible. Where that cannot be done the other bodies represented at the Convention must get together and arrange for Demonstrations.

Emphasis is laid upon the importance of Trades Councils and local Labour Parties **appointing deputations to attend branches of trade unions and workshop committees,** calling for support of the aims of the Leeds Convention and urging the appointment of delegates to the District Conferences.

The Provisional Committee will issue a Statement of Policy based upon the Resolutions passed at Leeds. The Statement will be issued with the invitation to attend the District Conferences.

District Conferences will deal with other business to be indicated later, when full particulars as to date, the precise place of meeting, &c., will be announced.

You are especially requested **to note that the District Conferences will be convened by the Provisional Committee** of the Workers' and Soldiers' Council now sitting in London.

It is urgently and imperatively requested that every person by whom this circular is read will send to the Secretary of the Workers' and Soldiers' Council, a list of all Labour, Socialist and Democratic Organisations, political and industrial, including Workshop Committees, Committees of Shop Stewards, and other working class organisations known to be established in any part of the country. Wherever possible, the names and addresses of the secretaries of these local bodies should be given.

The Provisional Committee of the Workers' and Soldiers' Council will then compile a complete list of all the bodies specified above, group them in accordance with the plan of territorial division, and then invite each organisation to appoint delegates to attend the District Conference.

All delegates to the Leeds Convention are urged to work through their organisations to secure co-ordination in promoting **Demonstrations** in support of the decisions of the Convention.

The exceptional facilities open to Trades Councils and local Labour Parties for the promotion of Demonstrations should be utilised to the fullest extent possible. Where that cannot be done the other bodies represented at the Convention must get together and arrange for Demonstrations.

Emphasis is laid upon the importance of Trades Councils and local Labour Parties **appointing deputations to attend branches of trade unions and workshop committees,** calling for support of the aims of the Leeds Convention and urging the appointment of delegates to the District Conferences.

The Provisional Committee will issue a Statement of Policy based upon the Resolutions passed at Leeds. The Statement will be issued with the invitation to attend the District Conferences.

In full and resolute confidence that Labour and Democracy will respond, we call for your enthusiastic aid for the great movement initiated at Leeds to restore peace, dethrone militarism, and to establish freedom.

Yours fraternally,

The Provisional Committee,

H. ALEXANDER	GEO. LANSBURY
CHAS. G. AMMON	J. RAMSAY MACDONALD
W. C. ANDERSON	TOM QUELCH
C. DESPARD	ROBERT SMILLIE
E. C. FAIRCHILD	PHILIP SNOWDEN
J. FINEBERG	ROBERT WILLIAMS
F. W. JOWETT	

All communications should be addressed to—

THE SECRETARY,

WORKERS' AND SOLDIERS' COUNCIL.

4 DUKE STREET, ADELPHI, LONDON, W.C.2.

Resolutions of the Leeds Convention

I.

Hail! The Russian Revolution

This Conference of Labour, Socialist and Democratic organisations of Great Britain hails the Russian Revolution! With gratitude and admiration it congratulates the Russian people upon a Revolution which has overthrown a tyranny that resisted the intellectual and social development of Russia, which has removed the standing menace of an aggressive imperialism in Eastern Europe, and which has liberated the people of Russia for the great work of establishing their own political and economic freedom on a firm foundation, and of taking a foremost part in the international movement for working-class emancipation from all forms of political, economic and imperialist oppression and exploitation.

II.

Foreign Policy and War Aims

This Conference of Labour, Socialist and Democratic organisations of Great Britain hails with the greatest satisfaction the declaration of the foreign policy and the war aims of the Russian Provisional Government, and it shares with them the firm conviction that the fall of Tsardom and the consolidation of democratic principles in Russia's internal and external policy will create in the democracies of other nations new aspirations towards a stable peace and the brotherhood of nations. In that belief we pledge ourselves to work for an agreement with the international democracies for the re-establishment of a general peace which shall not tend towards either domination by or over any nation, or the seizure of their national possessions, or the violent usurpation of their territories—a peace without annexations or indemnities and based on the rights of nations to decide their own affairs; and as a first step towards this aim we call upon the British Government immediately to announce its agreement with the declared foreign policy and war aims of the democratic Government of Russia.

III.

Civil Liberty

This Conference calls upon the Government of Great Britain to place itself in accord with the democracy of Russia by proclaiming its adherence to and determination to carry into immediate effect a charter of liberties establishing complete political rights for all men and women, unrestricted freedom of the press, freedom of speech, a general amnesty for all political and religious prisoners, full rights of industrial and political association, and the release of labour from all forms of compulsion and restraint.

IV.

Workmen's and Soldiers' Council

This Conference calls upon the constituent bodies at once to establish in every town, urban and rural district, Councils of Workmen's and Soldiers' Delegates for initiating and co-ordinating working-class activity in support of the policy set out in the foregoing resolutions, and to work strenuously for a peace made by the peoples of the various countries, and for the complete political and economic emancipation of international Labour. Such Councils shall also watch diligently for and resist every encroachment upon industrial and civil liberty; shall give special attention to the position of women employed in industry and generally support the work of the trade unions; shall take active steps to stop the exploitation of food and all other necessaries of life, and shall concern themselves with questions affecting the pensions of wounded and disabled soldiers and the maintenance grants payable to the dependents of men serving with the Army and Navy; and the making of adequate provision for the training of disabled soldiers and for suitable and remunerative work for the men on their return to civil life. And, further, that the conveners of this Conference be appointed a Provisional Committee, whose duty shall be to assist the formation of local Workmen's and Soldiers' Councils and generally to give effect to the policy determined by this Conference.

Printed at the National Labour Press Ltd., 8 & 9 Johnson's Court, Fleet Street, London, E.C.4

┌─────────────────────────────────────┐
│ ○   ○   │
│ ○   W O R K E R S'   A N D   ○   │
│ ○   S O L D I E R S' C O U N C I L │
│ ○   ○   │
└─────────────────────────────────────┘

MANIFESTO TO DISTRICT CONFERENCES

The memorable Leeds convention will remain a landmark in our democratic history. Masses of our people have been stirred deeply by the glorious Revolution achieved by the men and women of Russia. Caring for democracy and the Labour cause, with the triumph of which is bound up the triumph of world-wide peace, they have preserved the instinct of freedom through years of repressive and coercive laws. The time has come for organised common action, and for a general advance. The immediate outcome of the Leeds Convention was to band together lovers of freedom, so as to prevent the further loss of liberty, to recover the ground already lost, to attack Governmental and all other forms of tyranny, and to quicken the responsibility and power of democracy.

Democracy and Reaction

On all hands it was felt that the splendid enthusiasm of the Leeds Convention should not in any degree be dissipated. The future, as shaped by this world-shaking war and all its consequences, looms up, dim and uncertain, but with direct challenge to democracy. Reaction is strong now, and may be strong when the war is over. Hence men and women of good will, desiring a new Europe and a free humanity, cherishing a vision of a world redeemed from war and every form of oppression, must come together, and co-ordinate kindred organisations into one irresistible force.

The Work and the Spirit

Workers and soldiers are achieving a common power. If justice is to be secured for all soldiers and their dependents, and if freedom is to be won for all workers, they must join forces. These reasons led to the creation of the Workers' and Soldiers' Council. In accordance with the resolutions passed at Leeds, the Provisional Committee desires to indicate, in broad outline, to the local organisations something of the task ahead, and the spirit in which it should be undertaken.

The Russian Lead

Not in any narrow or exclusive sense, we desire to cultivate close alliance and solidarity with the Russian democracy. They have kindled in every land a new hope. They have given fresh courage to all struggling against bureaucracy and despotism and toward liberation. Every people must work out their own salvation in their own way, with such industrial and political weapons as may be available. The Russian workers have pointed the way towards the healing of nations and a new Internationalism, and it is the manifest duty of the Workers' and Soldiers' Council and all its branches to proclaim the real meaning and purpose of the Russian achievement, and its deep significance in relation to other countries, including our own. To celebrate the Russian Revolution, to welcome genuinely the dawn of freedom in that land, we must strengthen in our own country the movement toward political and industrial emancipation, and take a firm stand against all forms of exploitation.

The Breath of Revolution

The present hour, heavy with destiny and fate, with new mighty movements in the making, with the breath of revolution in the air, does not call immediately for programme-building, but when the full Council of 26 is assembled, and with the mandate from the Movement in the country, a full statement of immediate aims and objects will be forthcoming. Great principles are needed, and all should be inspired by the love of freedom, the hatred of tyranny. In all this, there is work lying ready to hand.

Then again, civil liberty and industrial freedom are more and more endangered the longer the war lasts, as the war drags out month after month, we witness the increasing taxation of the poor, the pressing into the army of the unfit, the breaking of pledges and promises, the growing bondage of labour, the gathering menace of industrial conscription. Civilisation itself is in gravest peril. The belligerent nations, under the impulse of passion, pursue a policy which in the end will wipe out one or two generations of men, pile up a vast debt, and indeed involve all of them in a common destruction. It is upon the workers that the burden will at last rest with most crushing force. Each country, therefore, must, clearly and without equivocation, define its foreign policy and war aims. Democratic Russia has written her aims honestly for the whole world to read.

The Doom of Rulers

Russia demands that democracy must rule, since the guilt and doom of rulers have been traced in the blood of millions. We are at one with Russia in striving for a people's peace. Russia urges us to work for the only stable and lasting peace—a peace born of the peoples, with the right of the people to decide their own future, with no violent usurpations or territorial aggression or annexations and indemnities which, though they may make irresistible appeal to diplomats, will heap up enormously the human slaughter, and prove fertile ground for future wars. It is our task to create such a volume of clear-thinking public opinion as will compel the British Government to fall into line with the Russian aims.

The Opportunity is Now

Our civil and industrial liberties, as by a flood, have been swept away under the pretext of the demands of war. Defence of the Realm Acts, Munition Acts, Conscription Acts, Orders in Council, have placed heavy shackles upon freedom of speech, freedom of conscience, freedom of the press, freedom of labour. A new charter of liberties has to be won. It must incorporate what was best in the past, and press forward to greater gains in the future. Labour must be free. Men and women must be able to speak the thing they believe true. General amnesty must be granted for political and religious prisoners. The blind, incompetent, stupid bureaucracy, under which the nation groans, must be utterly destroyed. The opportunity of the people is now. They must achieve their liberation, or remain fettered for long years to come. They must seize and retain the initiative, developing their own plans, pressing forward their own policies, not permitting themselves under all manner of specious pleas to be dragged in the wake of stupid coercion.

Organised Labour must be strengthened. Its outlook must be widened, through its ranks must spread the new restless spirit, pervading the world, demanding organic change. Profiteers and food gamblers, who have coined fortunes out of the waiting food queues and hungry necessities of the poor must be held up to public scorn, their shameful exploitation made impossible for all time to come.

We have to win justice for all soldiers and sailors and their dependents—adequate pensions, generous allowances, full provision and maintenance for the training of disabled men, proper safeguard for soldiers and sailors on their return to industrial life.

Workers and soldiers alike have trenches to defend and guard. The future of Britain is in their hands. Their interests are one and the greatest interest of all is freedom.

THE PROVISIONAL COMMITTEE OF THE WORKERS' AND SOLDIERS'
COUNCIL :—

H. ALEXANDER
CHAS. G. AMMON
W. C. ANDERSON, M.P.
C. DESPARD
E. C. FAIRCHILD
J. FINEBERG
F. W. JOWETT, M.P.

GEO. LANSBURY
J. RAMSAY MACDONALD, M.P.
TOM QUELCH
ROBERT SMILLIE
PHILIP SNOWDEN, M.P.
ROBERT WILLIAMS

All communications to the Secretary,
4, Duke Street, Adelphi, London, W.C. 2.

Printed at the National Labour Press, Ltd., 8 & 9 Johnson's Court, Fleet St., London, E.C.4

Afterword: The Leeds Convention at 100

Janet Douglas and Christian Høgsbjerg

The Leeds Convention at the Coliseum on 3 June 1917, when an estimated 3,500 people in total (including over 1,150 delegates) rallied in solidarity with the February Russian Revolution, clearly left powerful and abiding memories in all who attended, and the organisers themselves were thrilled at what they had accomplished.[46] Sylvia Pankhurst thought it 'splendid', and Charlotte Despard wrote of 'the wonder of Leeds'. As Philip Snowden put it in the *Labour Leader* on 7 June 1917, it had been a success 'far beyond the most sanguine expectations of the promoters. It was not only the largest Democratic Congress held in Great Britain since the days of the Chartist agitation' but a 'spontaneous expression of the spirit and enthusiasm of the Labour and Democratic movement'.[47] Writing about the Convention years later, in 1934, Snowden hailed it as 'the most democratically constituted Labour Convention ever held in this country … at that time railway travelling was very difficult, but no less than 1150 delegates came to the Convention hailing from every part of Britain … the great gallery of the theatre was crowded to suffocating with freely admitted visitors'.[48] For Fred Jowett, as Fenner Brockway noted, 'to the end of his life Fred used to refer to the Leeds Congress as the highest point of revolutionary fervour he had seen in this country'.[49]

The scholarly literature on the Leeds Convention is not vast, and indeed there is arguably still further work to be done. This is particularly so because, as memoirs by participants and newspaper reports of the event reveal, the transcripts of the speeches published in *What Happened at Leeds* (and republished in this booklet) are often slightly truncated versions of what was actually said, and it seems some of the more radical comments were cut out.[50] The extensive report in the *Leeds Weekly Citizen,* for example, notes the Convention began with the singing of *The Red Flag* 'with impressive force', and noted the messages of support including from 'the City of London Field Ambulance (F.Company) R[oyal].A[rmy].M[edical].C[orps]. stationed at Blackpool'.[51] Dora Montefiore recalled that MacDonald's 'speech was mainly a rhetorical indictment of Czarist Imperialism, and I was

105

able to point out, when seconding, that there were other Imperialisms as dangerous to the interests of the Proletarians of other countries as was that of Czardom. In fact, most of Mr. MacDonald's indictment might have been applied to British Imperialism.'[52] Montefiore in her speech, as recorded by the *Leeds Weekly Citizen,* did indeed include a fierce critique of imperialism:

> We know that the Powers are frightened of what is going on. Imperialism all over the world is shaking at its base. Every word said against Russian Imperialism applies to English Imperialism. We who have travelled know what Imperialism does for the native races all over the world. The new Imperialism is coming closer together and the Imperial Council is going to take all power away from the democracy and so as it chooses. You have to go and do what the Russian revolutionists have done.[53]

Edwin Fairchild in his speech began by stressing:

> We are here today to affirm that the working class is the only power which can make it unnecessary for armaments to be piled up, never of course piled up for aggression, but always we are told for defence. We are here to affirm that unless the working class move internationally along the lines laid down by our Russian comrades war will continue to claim the finest flower of the manhood of the nations.[54]

After Charles Roden Buxton had spoken, a delegate from East Fife in the gallery made an intervention from the floor:

> We ought to ask our Government immediately to resign, and let the people take charge, and declare ourselves here and now as the only means of maintaining peace throughout the world. What do the Russian people care about frontiers now? I passed a certain frontier for the first time on Saturday morning, and I didn't know I'd done it. Throw aside our old national ideas, explain our aims to Russia and Germany, and say we are ready here and now as an international Government to see to it that peace is maintained the world over.[55]

According to the *Nelson Leader*, at the end of his speech, Tom Mann declared 'When all the Allies were agreed to the Russian policy, if Germany still refused, then they might say, "see, there the evil lies!" But he did not think matters would end in that way, for though he had much reason to detest German militarism, having been expelled from

Germany by force many times, he had met thousands of men and women there whom he admired. At that point, cheers drowned out his words.'[56] According to the *Leeds Weekly Citizen*, Mann's very final words amid the cheers were his stating that 'he was an Internationalist when he was 30, and that day at 60, he was still an Internationalist'.[57] Sylvia Pankhurst 'hoped the representation of women [on the future provisional committee of the Workers' and Soldiers' Council established by the Convention] would not be limited to one in 13, for in point of view of numbers women preponderated to the extent of 13 to 12 men, not one in 13 men'.[58] Other interventions missing from the final official transcript of conference proceedings came from a Russian-born Jewish activist, Solly Abrahams, while after Bertrand Russell's speech, 'an Irishwoman, speaking from the body of the hall, asked that the condition of Ireland should be remembered at this moment. The people of Ireland looked for help to British democracy'. At the close of the event, after deciding to elect representatives from thirteen districts across the country, Robert Smillie declared 'This ought not to be done nine months hence, but at the earliest possible moment', which was agreed. 'Hearty cheers were given for International Socialism, and with the singing of *The Red Flag* the Congress ended'.[59]

Aside from odd mentions in memoirs by participants, the first wave of literature on the Leeds Convention came in 1967, in the aftermath of the fiftieth anniversary of the Russian Revolution (and so of the Leeds Convention itself), and amid the high point of post-war class struggle in Britain which followed from the late 1960s into the early 1970s.[60] As well as Ken Coates's introduction (reprinted in the present volume), Stephen White in 1974 published what still in many ways remains the most detailed historical account of the Convention, an article entitled 'Soviets in Britain: The Leeds Convention of 1917' in the *International Review of Social History*. White's argument – contra Jowett - was that the Convention is best understood 'in a pacifist than a revolutionary perspective'. *The Times* on 4 June 1917 commented that the object of the Leeds Convention was to 'stop the war', and only after this objective was achieved would organisers embark upon any 'domestic [class] war'. White quotes George Lansbury stating in *The Herald* in September 1917 that there should be a 'more excellent method of securing Labour's aims' than revolution, and the Workmen's and Soldiers' Councils should serve as a 'unifying force throughout the land, drawing to themselves all the men and women who wish to work for a better Britain after the war and an early peace'.[61]

It is indeed striking one hundred years on, when we commemorate the centenary of the First World War, just how important the Convention – sometimes described as the 'Leeds Peace Convention' — was in terms of its stance on the war. It was perhaps the biggest explicitly 'anti-war' gathering held in Britain during the war. As Bertrand Russell testified about his intervention relating to the Conscientious Objectors (CO's) in a private letter on 5 June 1917,

> To my great surprise, they gave me about the greatest ovation that was given to anybody. I got up to speak, and they shouted for me to go on the platform, and when I got there they cheered endlessly. They applauded everything that had to do with CO's – Allen's name came up often, and always produced a great cheer.[62]

Yet matters are complicated. As David Howell notes, 'certainly, practically no one argued for revolutionary defeatism', and 'a much more common response' among the British Left and labour movement in general in this period 'was not so much opposition to British involvement than an attempt to mitigate the illiberality of the state and typically a desire to end the war as soon as possible'.

> The underlying outlook for many Liberals and socialists was that the war was not so much an opportunity for radical advance as an interruption in the advance of Progress. It is in this context that the popular mood in 1917 should be interpreted and it is important to remember that the February Revolution could be used by pro-war elements to polish their democratic credentials.[63]

Moreover, to downplay the revolutionary dimension to proceedings seems to us mistaken, as the Leeds Convention, with its celebration of the February Russian Revolution and attempts to emulate the Workers', Peasants' and Soldiers' Councils in Petrograd, struck a real chord in the British working class. Certainly, press reports often made the link between revolution at home and the ending of the war.[64] On the same day as the Leeds Convention was held, the local ILP branch in Briton Ferry in Wales organised an open-air meeting to celebrate the Russian

Revolution, aimed at those who could not make the trip to Leeds. At the end of the meeting they unanimously adopted the same four resolutions discussed at Leeds, and then several mass 'report-back' meetings were held across South Wales to hear about the Convention. On 16 June, for example, Tom Mann addressed 2,000 people at the Rink in Merthyr on the Russian Revolution, the Leeds Convention and 'Trade Unionism after the War' and a vote was taken unanimously to endorse the four resolutions. As the local paper, *The Pioneer,* notes, this rally revealed 'Leeds was but a reflex of Merthyr and of every progressive industrial centre'. On 2 July, Mann spoke to another mass rally of 1,000 people at Ynyshir and then 2,000 in Porth. As *The Pioneer* noted at the end of the Ynyshir rally, 'three cheers for Russia were given with such force and volume, as I did believe have never been heard in this town before. Working-class solidarity throughout the world was, everyone believed, the only counter to imperialistic aggression and capitalistic greed resulting in wars and the destruction of the proletariat'.[65] By the end of July 1917, a link was being made between Lenin, who had by now raised in Russia the slogan 'All Power to the Soviets' (and was busy writing his classic analysis of the soviets, *The State and Revolution*) and some of those home-grown *Lennites*, who supported the Leeds Convention. The *Leeds Mercury,* for example, on 27 July 1917 wrote of Lenin – describing him as a paid German agent and 'a vile traitor to Russian liberties' - as 'the trusted idol of these people'.[66]

Overall, as Donny Gluckstein put it in 1985,

> The Leeds Convention was the first of several abortive attempts in Western Europe to create workers' councils under the control of official labour leaders. Genuine workers' councils could not be built from the top downwards in this way. They were generated by the self-activity of the rank and file coupled with the willingness of militants to lead their struggle in a political direction. Only Gallacher, the Clyde Workers' Committee representative at Leeds, showed any understanding of the Russian example, because he had worked in a movement which had started in the road towards the soviet. He alone suggested the workers' council as an alternative form of state to bourgeois parliament, urging the Convention 'not to resurrect a dead House of Commons, but aided by the Workers' Committee, carry through the revolution by taking over the control and direction of all that goes to make up the life of the nation.'[67]

The idea of 'Western Soviets' forming was not a pipedream, but became a reality across Europe in many countries in the revolutionary wave sparked by the October Revolution in Russia. Even in Britain, as John Newsinger puts it, 'if the war had continued beyond 1918 and into 1919, there is no doubt there would have been a serious crisis at home'.

> [I]f Britain had been defeated in the German spring offensive in 1918, this would have certainly precipitated the downfall of the Saxe-Coburg-Gotha dynasty (they had cunningly changed their name to Windsor during war!), just as German defeat was to precipitate the downfall of their cousins, the Hohenzollerns. Indeed, on 11 November, Douglas Haig, the British commander-in-chief in France, actually noted in his diary that 'the Kaiser is in Holland' and that 'if the war had gone against us no doubt our king would have had to go' and it would have been the British army in a state of mutiny instead of the German ... there was a very real fear in ruling circles in 1917-1918 that the war was going to end in revolution.[68]

In this sense, given the fears that the Russian Revolution still conjures up in the minds of the rich and powerful the world over, perhaps it is not surprising that the Leeds Convention is not better known and better remembered. Reading and re-reading its discussions, resolutions, speeches and arguments today reminds us of the relevance and potential appeal of revolutionary democratic and socialist ideas at a time of crisis, war and tumult. The Leeds Convention as a whole deserves be remembered as an inspiration for us today, and a remarkable moment of internationalism and solidarity in the history of the working class movement in Britain.

Contributors

Ken Coates (1930-2010) was a miner and adult educator. His many books include an acclaimed history of the founding of the TGWU, *The Making of the Labour Movement*, co-authored with Tony Topham (Spokesman, 1994). Ken worked with Bertrand Russell from 1965 until Russell's death in 1970, after which he ran the Bertrand Russell Peace Foundation to continue Russell's work for peace, human rights and social justice. Ken helped found the Institute for Workers' Control in 1968. He was twice expelled from the Labour Party, by Wilson in the 1960s and by Blair in the 1990s. For ten years from 1989, Ken was an elected Member of the European Parliament, where he chaired the Human Rights Committee and organised two Full Employment Conventions, the Pensioners' Parliament, and the Disabled People's Parliament. He died in 2010.

Janet Douglas was a principal lecturer in Politics at what is now Leeds Becketts University. Since her retirement, she is an independent scholar with a range of research interests including the history of Leeds and architectural history.

Christian Høgsbjerg is an independent historian who works as administrator for Leeds University Centre for African Studies. He is the author of *C.L.R. James in Imperial Britain*, and is the editor of a new special edition of C.L.R. James's 1937 pioneering anti-Stalinist history of the Comintern, *World Revolution, 1917-1936: The Rise and Fall of the Communist International* (both with Duke University Press). He is a member of the editorial board of *International Socialism*.

Notes

1 The Leeds socialist and suffragist Isabella Ford (1855-1924) sat on the Society's committee and the Leeds branch of the Society was particularly active.

2 Philip Viscount Snowden, *An Autobiography, Volume One, 1864-1919* (London: Ivor Nicholson and Watson, 1934), 447-448. For an interesting report of the speech O'Grady gave in Leeds on his return from revolutionary Russia, see *Leeds Weekly Citizen*, 15 June 1917. O'Grady would later go on to become Governor of Tasmania and then of the Falklands for which services he was knighted.

3 *The Herald*, 31 March 1917.

4 'The Revolt at the Albert Hall', *The Herald*, 7 April 1917.

5 *The Herald*, 28 April 1917. See also https://www2.warwick.ac.uk/services/library/mrc/explorefurther/digital/russia/menshevik/

6 *Labour Leader*, 10 May 1917, quoted in Alan Clinton and George Myers, 'The Russian Revolution and the British working class – two episodes', *Fourth International*, 4, 3 (November 1967).

7 See *Leeds Weekly Citizen*, 4 May 1917; *Leeds Weekly Citizen* 11 May 1917; *Yorkshire Post* 7 May 1917. Thanks to Iain Dalton for this information.

8 *The Herald*, 12 May 1917.

9 *The Herald*, 12 May 1917.

10 Reproduced in Snowden, *An Autobiography*, 450-452.

11 'Great labour, socialist and democratic convention to hail the Russian Revolution and to organise the British democracy To follow Russia (circular)', 23 May 2017, Postal and Telegraph Clerks' Association 148/PA/2/5/2/3, Modern Records Centre, University of Warwick, online at: http://contentdm.warwick.ac.uk/cdm/ref/collection/russian/id/516

12 See Stephen White, 'Soviets in Britain: the Leeds convention of 1917', *International Review of Social History*, 19, 2 (1974), 184.

13 Snowden, *An Autobiography*, 452. For example, the *Yorkshire Evening Post* on 31 May denounced the Convention under the headline 'Using the City to preach Sedition' whilst its sister paper, the *Yorkshire Post* stressed in their reports that the conference had been planned in London and had had nothing to do with the Labour Party and Trade Unions in Leeds.

14 Quoted in Walter Kendall, *The Revolutionary Movement in Britain, 1900-1921: The Origins of British Communism* (London: Weidenfeld and Nicolson, 1969), 175.

15 See White, 'Soviets in Britain: the Leeds convention of 1917', 172. The Leeds Trades Council met on the 30 May and voted 37 to 30 to send three

delegates to the Convention. A day later the Leeds Labour Party decided by a vote of 75 to 15 to send two delegates. Both organisations also voted that a fifth resolution be discussed at the Convention calling on German workers to rid themselves of their despotic government. The organisers of the Convention however kept a firm control over the Convention's proceedings, disallowing any additional resolutions.

16 Thanks to Darren Treadwell for this information.

17 *The Herald*, 2 June 1917.

18 'The Lead from Leeds', *The Herald*, 2 June 1917. In *Forward*, 2 June 1917, Snowden is also quoted the day before the Convention as saying 'this next weekend should see Great Britain painted red'. See White, 'Soviets in Britain: the Leeds convention of 1917', 172. See also George Lansbury, 'Wake Up, England!' *The Herald*, 26 May 1917 and Robert Williams, 'Internationalism', *The Herald*, 26 May 1917 for how they envisaged the tasks of the Leeds Convention.

19 *Yorkshire Post*, 4 June 1917. Both the Leeds Institute and the Coliseum are still standing, the former is now the City Museum whilst the Coliseum is the 02 Academy (and before that the Town and Country Club). For a report of the Convention's evening rally, see the *Leeds Weekly Citizen*, 8 June 1917.

20 'What Happened at Leeds', *The Herald*, 9 June 1917.

21 Online at the Marxists Internet Archive: https://www.marxists.org/history/international/social-democracy/1917/ leeds-guardian.htm

22 The organisers of the Stockholm Peace Conference issued invitations to Socialist delegates from all belligerent countries including Germany. In August 1914 following much press lobbying, the British Government announced that passports would not be issued to travel to Stockholm. The Conference never took place.

23 For more on this, see Fenner Brockway, *Socialism over Sixty Years: The Life of Jowett of Bradford* (London: George Allen and Unwin, 1946), 154-156.

24 Norman and Jeanne MacKenzie (eds.), *The Diary of Beatrice Webb, Vol. 3: 1905-1924 'The Power to Alter Things'* (London: Virage and the L.S.E., 1984), 281.

25 White, 'Soviets in Britain: the Leeds convention of 1917', 176. Even the *Yorkshire Evening Post* noted on 21 July 1917 of the lack of unity amongst delegates to the Provisional Committee of the Workmen's and Soldiers' Council, 'the ILP wanted state socialism, the BSP a communist state, the UDC crowd would be satisfied with a modified capitalism on a Republican basis, the Shop Stewards and syndicalists wanted a syndicalist country'.

26 White, 'Soviets in Britain: the Leeds convention of 1917', 176-177.

Pankhurst's journal, *Women's Dreadnought*, recommended the Councils be renamed 'Workers', Soldiers' and Housewives' Councils'.

27 White, 'Soviets in Britain: the Leeds convention of 1917', 178.

28 White, 'Soviets in Britain: the Leeds convention of 1917', 178-179, 182-183.

29 Griffin, Nicholas (ed.) *A Pacifist at War: Letters and Writings of Bertrand Russell, 1914-1918* (Nottingham: Spokesman, 2014), 122.

30 White, 'Soviets in Britain: the Leeds convention of 1917', 186. As Snowden put it bluntly later, 'It may be, I do not rule it out of theoretical consideration, that Workers' and Soldiers' Councils or Soviets may come to Britain but I am for Socialism coming through parliament and no other way'. Quoted in J.T. Murphy, *New Horizons* (London: The Bodley Head, 1941), 62.

31 See John Newsinger, *Them and Us: Fighting the Class War 1910-1939* (London: Bookmarks, 2015), 56-57.

32 Quoted in J.H. Winter, *Socialism and the challenge of war: ideas and politics in Britain, 1912-18* (London: Routledge and K. Paul, 1974), 239.

33 Mary Agnes Hamilton, quoted in Newsinger, *Them and Us*, 61.

34 Snowden, *An Autobiography*, 456. As early as 5 June, the *Morning Post* and the *Daily Telegraph* published strongly-worded articles urging the Government to take steps to stop the operations of the Peace Convention referring to delegates as 'wreckers' set on creating anarchy in the country. Other press tactics were to refer to the Convention as 'a bogus conference' whose delegates lacked bone fide credentials. According to James O' Grady the pro-war Leeds Labour MP some unions were not even invited to send delegates, and Ben Tillett stated that at least 500 delegates were under the age of 26 with the clear inference that they were 'draft-dodgers'. According to Will Thorne, two members of the ILP had scoured the East End of London to find Jewish delegates to attend the Convention. *Yorkshire Post,* 7 June 1917 and 26 July 1917.

35 White, 'Soviets in Britain: the Leeds convention of 1917', 179.

36 White, 'Soviets in Britain: the Leeds convention of 1917', 184-186.

37 Quoted in Christopher Draper, 'The Leeds Soviet 1917', *Northern Voices*, (January 2017), http://northernvoicesmag.blogspot.co.uk/2017/01/the-leeds-soviet-1917.html

38 White, 'Soviets in Britain: the Leeds convention of 1917', 192-193.

39 On the riot, see Snowden, *An Autobiography*, 456. For more on the ill-fated attempt to spread the workers' council movement after Leeds, see White, 'Soviets in Britain: the Leeds convention of 1917', 188-190 and Draper, 'The Leeds Soviet 1917'.

40 Griffin (ed.) *A Pacifist at War*, 128-129.
41 See David Egan, 'The Swansea Conference of the British Council of Soldiers' and Workers' Delegates, July 1917: Reactions to the Russian Revolution of February, 1917, and the Anti-War Movement in South Wales', *Llafur*, 1, 4 (1975), 12, 23. Thanks to Stuart Staunton for alerting us to this essay.
42 See *Yorkshire Evening Post*, 26 July 1917 *Yorkshire Post*, 5 August and 21 August 1917 and *Leeds Mercury*, 22 August 1917.
43 White, 'Soviets in Britain: the Leeds convention of 1917', 191-193.
44 Council of Workers' and Soldiers' Delegates, 'Workers' and Soldiers' Council: Leeds Convention (circular)', 15 June 1917. From Modern Records Centre, University of Warwick, [Postal and Telegraph Clerks' Association, 148/PA/2/5/2/2], online at http://contentdm.warwick.ac.uk/cdm/ref/collection/russian/id/515
45 Council of Workers' and Soldiers' Delegates, 'Manifesto to District Conferences (circular)', Modern Records Centre, University of Warwick, Papers of Percy Collick, Correspondence and ephemera, c.1917-1931, 379/PC/6/4/13.
46 White, 'Soviets in Britain: the Leeds convention of 1917', 173. For the estimate of 3,500 people, see the *Leeds Weekly Citizen*, 8 June 1917.
47 Quoted in White, 'Soviets in Britain: the Leeds convention of 1917', 175.
48 Snowden, *An Autobiography*, 452. Snowden suggested that, despite the press hysteria about the event, 'There was not the slightest evidence of any opposition either inside the theatre or among the crowds outside. The delegates went about the streets wearing their red ribbons without the slightest molestation'. However, as we have seen already this was not quite the case. According to Bertrand Russell, on the way to the Convention MacDonald was fearful that the Convention would not take place as 'we should be broken up by soldiers'. See Griffin (ed.) *A Pacifist at War*, 122. Indeed, the evening of 3 June and 4 June 1917 did see major anti-semitic race riots in the predominantly Jewish area of the Leylands (bordered by North Street and Regent Street) in Leeds; during the Jewish influx of the 1890s from places like Russia and later, most immigrants (especially the poorer ones) had settled here and the district was colloquially referred to as the 'Leeds Jewish ghetto'. Alf Mattison thought the two matters were completely unconnected, but the possible relationship between the presence in the city of patriotic proto-fascist elements whipped up in advance to attack the Leeds Convention, their failure to achieve this aim, and then the anti-semitic race riots against Russian Jews in the city that evening needs further investigation. As Colin Holmes asks, were Jewish people 'the

scapegoats for hostility which otherwise might have been directed against the Socialists? Such a suggestion has been made but no 'hard' evidence has been adduced in its support.' See Colin Holmes, *Anti-Semitism in British Society, 1876-1939* (Abingdon: Routledge, 2015), 137. One figure who tried to inform various authorities including the Petrograd Soviet itself about these riots after witnessing them first hand was 'Abraham Bezalel' (a Russian-born Jewish activist called Solly Abrahams), who had earlier spoken at the Leeds Convention where he was described as 'Mr. Bezalel', who gave 'an eloquent plea' for 'the Russians in England who are to be conscribed [conscripted]'. See 'What Happened at Leeds', *The Herald*, 9 June 1917.

49 Brockway, *Socialism over Sixty Years*, 153.

50 Even the original *Herald* account contains more details of how the event ran itself, with Margaret Bondfield for example speaking on behalf of the Standing Orders Committee, and how the Convention voted by a large majority to discuss only the resolutions on the agenda, despite protestations and attempt at amendments on the part of Edward Tupper of the Seamen's Union, Hartlepool Labour League and DB Foster of Leeds Trades Council. See 'What happened at Leeds', *The Herald*, 9 June 1917. Tupper's 1938 autobiography gives a very vivid sense of his contribution and the turmoil in proceedings it created – including an apparently violent altercation with Solly Abrahams. See Edward Tupper, *Seamen's Torch: The life story of Captain Edward Tupper, National Union of Seamen* (London: The National Book Association / Hutchinsons, 1938), 185-187.

51 'The National Socialist Convention', *Leeds Weekly Citizen*, 8 June 1917.

52 Dora Montefiore, *From a Victorian to a Modern* (London: E. Archer, 1927), 194.

53 'The National Socialist Convention', *Leeds Weekly Citizen*, 8 June 1917.

54 'The National Socialist Convention', *Leeds Weekly Citizen*, 8 June 1917.

55 'The National Socialist Convention', *Leeds Weekly Citizen*, 8 June 1917.

56 *Nelson Leader*, 10 and 17 August 1917, quoted in Joseph White, *Tom Mann* (Manchester: Manchester University Press, 1991), 192.

57 'The National Socialist Convention', *Leeds Weekly Citizen*, 8 June 1917.

58 'The National Socialist Convention', *Leeds Weekly Citizen*, 8 June 1917.

59 'What happened at Leeds', *The Herald*, 9 June 1917.

60 See for example, for the CPGB, the brief celebratory discussion in R. Page Arnot, *The Impact of the Russian Revolution in Britain* (London: Lawrence and Wishart, 1967), 63-65, and the more critical analysis in Clinton and Myers, 'The Russian Revolution and the British working class', Kendall, *The Revolutionary Movement in Britain*, 174-176, and also Ray Challinor,

The Origins of British Bolshevism (London: Croom Helm, 1977), 180-183.

61 White, 'Soviets in Britain: the Leeds convention of 1917', 166, 182.

62 Griffin (ed.) *A Pacifist at War*, 122.

63 David Howell, personal communication with Christian Høgsbjerg, 23 March 2017.

64 *Yorkshire Evening Post*, 21 July 1917.

65 Egan, 'The Swansea Conference of the British Council of Soldiers' and Workers' Delegates, July, 1917', 17-18.

66 For a recollection of how Lenin gradually became better known during 1917 among militant workers in Britain, see Harry McShane and Joan Smith, *No Mean Fighter* (London: Pluto, 1978), 89-90.

67 Donny Gluckstein, *The Western Soviets: Workers' Councils versus Parliament, 1915-1920* (London: Bookmarks, 1985), 81. Gallacher's comments were in *The Call*, paper of the BSP, 28 December 1917.

68 Newsinger, *Them and Us*, 60-61.

British Labour
and the
Russian
Revolution

The Leeds Convention:
a report from the
Daily Herald
with an Introduction
by Ken Coates

Documents on Socialist History: No. 1   Published by Spokesman Books

Price: 40p

Cover of the 1974 edition